In the same series

Recent Commonwealth Literature (2 vols.)
R.K. Dhawan, A.K. Shrivastava and P.V. Dhamija, ed.

New Zealand Literature Today
R.K. Dhawan and Walter Tonetto, ed.

Australian Literature Today
R.K. Dhawan and David Kerr, ed.

Australian Literature and Indian Literature: Studies in Mutual Response
David Kerr and R.K. Dhawan, ed.

A.D. Hope: Questions of Poetic Strength
Walter Tonetto

South Asian Responses to Chinua Achebe
Bernth Lindfors and Bala Kothandaraman, ed.

Indian Response to African Writing
A. Ramakrishna Rao and C.R.Visweswara Rao , ed.

The Novels of Ayi Kwei Armah
K. Damodar Rao

The Novels of Wole Soyinka
M. Rajeshwar

The Novels of V.S. Naipaul
Shashi Kamra

Commonwealth Writing

A Study in Expatriate Experience

Edited by
R.K. Dhawan
L.S.R. Krishna Sastry

PRESTIGE

Published by
Prestige Books
New Delhi 110 008

1994
ISBN: 81-85218-82-X

Phototypesetting by
Pivot Computers
Delhi 110 006
Ph. 291 8404

Printed at
Mehra Offset Press
Delhi 110 002

Contents

Fiction

Poetry

Contributors

Jose Alilakuzhy, Newman College, Thodupuzha

Vandana Datta, Patna

A. Hariprasanna, S.V. University, Tirupati

F.A. Inamdar, South Gujarat University, Surat

S. Indira, Dr. L.B. College, Visakhapatnam

Novy Kapadia, University of Delhi

Manjushree S. Kumar, Jodhpur

Kai Nicholson, University of Poona

Indira Nityanandam, Navgujarat College, Ahmedabad

D.K. Pabby, University of Delhi

T. Padma, Andhra University, Visakhapatnam

V.S. Patel, Arts and Commerce College, Chanasma

Z.N. Patil, University of Poona

M. Rajeshwar, Kakatiya University, Warangal

K.V. Rama Rao, S.K.V.T. College, Rajahmundry

Shobha Shinde, Jai Hind College, Dhule

G.K. Subbarayudu, O.U. College for Women, Hyderabad

S. Sujatha, Andhra University, Visakhapatnam

C. Vijayasree, Osmania University, Hyderabad

Are We Expatriates?

KAI NICHOLSON

Are we not all expatriates? Yes and No. A dubious answer, not cut and dry and wholly unacademic; nevertheless, justified.

For the greater number of the Commonwealth's citizens, English remains to an extent, outside the sphere of their daily lives. They have no need for it. How many of us in the Commonwealth of Nations, comprising of about 1.2 billions or more, depend on English? Not many, but it still is an important factor in keeping the nations' wheels of administration moving, the courts working, the hospitals dispensing and caring, the schools and colleges teaching. But even though the numbers of those who master English are as yet small in comparison with those millions of people who speak, read and write in the myriad other languages, this one manner of speech has become the language of the rising middle classes. It is their passport to what they consider success, security and affluency.

And of all the countries in the Commonwealth, India has the largest number of English speaking people: about 68 millions. And if more and more people want to master English, is it only because it is a vehicle to ensure them a better life? Nothing more? There's the rub.

At this point I'd like to turn to India. And it is in the urban setting where we live and work in the nuclei of English-speaking people. Their education is still British, and also to a certain extent their life-styles, with Americanisms permeating from the upper to the middle classes. In a recent article in *The Sunday Times of India,* the sons and daughters of these families were described as absorbing with an uncritical approach much of what is available of the Anglo-Saxon civilization. Evidently, their reading habits are formed by the influences of this civilization, partly by their education and partly by their interest, and when they read Indo-English literature, it is because the plots and characters are urban, and in tune with their thought-patterns. It reflects, scrutinizes, criticizes, analyzes their particular environment, and of course the world around them, even if it means that they do not directly identify themselves as a full part of it. It is participation, but at arms length. Of course the writers themselves are working within these nuclei, and some of them who do project their thoughts from the point of view of an outsider, are still caught in the web of "Orwell's dilemma." The struggle of breaking out of the orbit, but not quite making it.

Now I ask: Is the anglicized-Indian an expatriate? By this I mean a person who has just adopted the English language for whatever reason. The answer could be no, since India possesses an ethnic and cultural diversity greater than Europe's and of the Middle East together, and so the miniscule anglicized-Indian could be absorbed. Yes, if the Anglo-Saxon culture is decidedly taken as a foreign body. It is a complex situation; take it a step further: an anglicized Punjabi, and a writer of English verse in Kerala. Would he consider himself an expatriate? Ethnically, there is no doubt, but not if he communicates with the likes of him. Then he would be an expatriate of the second order; that is, at sea once out of reach of the like-minded.

I shall not dwell on this aspect any further, but it would be interesting to know, if such problems can also be associated with other essentially non-English-speaking members of the Commonwealth.

The traditional terminology is the writer living and working abroad. One of the reasons for this situation, and which occurs most often, is self-imposed exile, due to a writer's difficulty in identifying him/herself with a government, or a feeling of non-acceptance by a society to which he/she may belong. I often ask myself, how does the expatriate writer remain in the mainstream of life away from home for long period of time? In his world frozen? I recall how Alexander Solzhenitsyn failed to grip the attention of the non-communist world after his deportation. In the intellectual isolation in Vermont, cut off from the Russian heart, his mind dried up. Other writers in a similar situation were lost to themselves once they were unable to breath the air of their natural environment: like Stefan Zweig, who committed suicide in South America when the Nazis began their purge of the intellectuals. But there were others too who left Germany's shores during those dark years: the brothers Thomas and Heinrich Mann, Bertolt Brecht and Erich Maria Remarque to name a few. These writers spent the war years in the United States, but mentally they were expatriates who held on to ideologies in which they believed and which they fought for during their exile, with the hope, the wish and the desire to see these bloom after the holocaust. Heinrich Mann and Bertolt Brecht returned, and chose the socialist East Germany, Thomas Mann and Remarque saw the chance of the pursuance of the ideals in Western Europe. All four of them believed that the country, now freed from the clutches of National Socialism, would provide them with the basis from which they could develop their particular intellects and writings. But as we know too well, Germany after 1945, both East and West, was not the Germany that came into being after World War I. The Weimar Republic was dead, and that nation's successors were not interested in revivalism. Undoubtedly, the works of these men are classics of literature, but they reflect an age now vanished.

Coming back to our Commonwealth, I'd like to take up the Indian author, Rohinton Mistry, settled in Canada for more than a decade. His works: *Tales from Firozshah Baug* and *Such a Long Journey* deal with his past, a Bombay he left behind. However, Mistry's Indian world will stop growing unless he returns and plunges back into Bombay's hybrid culture. Of course, he could continue to write in the present vein, but after a while the vividness of his world can start fading, and imagination will replace realism. I am in no way discounting the power and beauty of imagination, but in the case of Mistry, where his novels are so full of documentation, this aspect will, I think, be frozen to his time in India. There is of course the possibility, and a strong one at that, of gathering news and views of his homeland through the media, members of his community in Canada, and correspondence; but all this information which he would store in the archive of his mind, could all help evolve a new set of moods, closer to present-day India than his previous work, but would they have the same intensity? Can imagination divorced of experience give the reader the sense of a real presence? I would say, it would be very difficult.

In my opinion V.S. Naipaul's best piece of writing has been his *A House for Mr Biswas* and secondary to it, his controversial documentaries: *An Area of Darkness* and *India: A Wounded Civilisation.* But of the latter, I wonder if they have not been studies of himself and his place in the country of his forefathers than of India itself. Both works are those of self-identification. Was he in India as an expatriate, or did he try to find himself back to where he spiritually belonged, but was unable to adjust his mind and his emotions to the incompatibilities which lay bare before him. To me it seems that India's social and historical fabric, taking them for what they are rather what they should be, did not fit in with his pre-fabricated emotions. Here I would like to put the question: Naipaul analyzed the scenes before him, but did he understand them? And if these documentaries found praise in the West, was it because he interpreted India with the perception of a European mind; a mind habituated by certain categorical depictions?

And then there is, of course, Nirad Chaudhuri. He is a personality no one can get by, even if in a form of a reference. Volumes could be written about this extraordinary gentleman, but what I have read makes me feel that he is closer to England than he is to the country of his birth. He is an expatriate in India, writing about India and her history with Britain, but his heart was always, if I may use Orwell's phrase, "in this green and pleasant land."

With heart and soul in England, but both feet on the ground in India has been, or still is, a case for study, for the problems they create lingers on in the minds of expatriates in India. Ruth Jhabvala's English characters have difficulty in finding peace of mind in post-colonial India. In "Myself in India" in her collection of stories in *Out of India,* she is hesitant, but she doesn't shy away from the problem. "And here, it seems to me, I come to the heart of my problem. To live in India and be at peace, one must to a very considerable extent become Indian and adopt Indian attitudes, habits, beliefs, assume if possible an Indian personality. But how is this possible? And even if it were possible—without cheating oneself—would it be desirable? Should one want to try to become something other than what one is? I don't always say no to this question. Sometimes it seems to me how pleasant it would be to say yes and give in and wear a sari and be meek and accepting and see God in a cow. Other times it seems worthwhile to be defiant and European and all right, be crushed by one's environment, but all the same have made some attempt to remain standing. Of course this can't go on indefinitely and in the end I'm bound to lose—if only at the point where my ashes are immersed in the Ganges to the accompaniment of Vedic hymns, and then who will say that I have not truly merged with India?"

This is the question, I think, Naipaul should ask himself, if he wishes to decide to accept the reality of India. Otherwise his West-Indian novel will remain his best.

In this context I want to mention E.M. Forster's *A Passage to*

India only to point out a similarity between his Mrs. Moore and Fielding and Jhabvala's Europeans.

The attitudes just mentioned have a historical linkage. Allen J. Greenberger's critical study *A British Image of India* puts us through the thought-processes of the English in India. In the chapters dealing with the Era of Doubt (1910-1935) and the Era of Melancholy (1935-1960) the authors work in two perspectives: they are not sure if it is possible to have successful relationship between the Indians and the British; and though they express love for India, they feel that the people of this country no longer need them. Preceding despondency and disillusionment comes the Era of Confidence (1880-1910). Rudyard Kipling's *Kim* moves around in a stable society. "The British Raj," writes Christopher Hollis in "Kim the apolitical Man," "was established and taken for granted. Subversive movements and foreign intrigues on the frontier might be introduced in order to make the plot of a story exciting. But there was no question of such movement succeeding or changing the nature of society." And this was possible, as the historian Michael Edwardes writes in "Rudyard Kipling and the Imperial Imagination," because the British felt that it was their duty to be in India. "It was simply a necessity imposed upon England by some gigantic determinism." Much of this missionary zeal was fanned by John Ruskin in 1870, when he appealed to young Englishmen to go out beyond the shores of Britain and paint the world red. Many English novelists in India ardently held the Union Jack high. Flora Annie Steel, Bithia Mae Croker, Ethel M. Dell, Maud Driver, Hugh S. Scott, A.E.W. Mason, G.A. Henty and many others portrayed English characters, men and women, who were tough, duty-bound, unflinching when faced by difficult tasks, full of bravado and recklessness, but conscious of their race and cultural superiority. There is no doubt that Social-Darwinism played a major part in the novelists' projection of their characters in India. These expatriate writers were part of Kipling's pack. "Rather death than stepping out of line," as Croker writes in *Mutiny Lady*. But the British, as expatriate writers described them, took their work seriously, though today their opinions would be unacceptable.

Greenberger has this to say: "The foremost trait of the Indians is that they are like little children. This is a statement which holds true for all the Indians of the British writers in this period who apply it to virtually all Indians with whom they deal. . . . The image of the Indian as a child fitted in very nicely with the British image of himself as a strong all-knowing leader. . . . The British obviously, according to these authors, knew what was right for the Indians just as a father would for his children. . . . By right of race the Briton was the leader and father and the Indian the follower and child. Any attempt to upset this was to go against the rules of nature." But despite confidence in the mission of empire, in the very era when Englishmen believed themselves the masters of India's destiny, doubt crept in. Said William Hunter in *The Old Missionary:* "The Englishman in India has no home and leaves no memory."

Is this the struggle of the ex-patriate writer whether in India or abroad? Paul Scott's characters in the *Raj Quartet* and subsequent novels on post-colonial India seem to leave little trace of their being in India except in old and tumbled-down graveyards strewn across the vast sub-continent. Similarly, Manohar Malgonkar's *Combat of Shadows*. Here is a picture of the decline of Edwardian English middle class with an imperial backdrop – India of the Raj.

Anita Desai is not an expatriate, but her past is. In *Baumgartner's Bombay* her mother's past and hers are relevant in this novel. I am not implying that Baumgartner is affiliated to their lives; but the life and death of this German Jew, a refugee from Nazi terror, is close to reality. Baumgartner, son of a wealthy furniture dealer, runs away from Berlin before Hitler's henchmen have turned the whole of Germany into a vast concentration camp. Baumgartner and other exiles lead listless lives in India and end up in the squalor of Bombay's Colaba. They are haunted by their past, and go through the nightmare of Nazi persecution, and when they shake it off, for a while, they return to their childhood, the happy days full of sunshine and laughter, before the jackboots of the SS and SA tramped through the streets of Berlin. Symbolically, Baumgartner's German past catches up with him. He befriends a young German: "A German from Germany. Baumgartner had sensed, he had smelt the German in him like a cat might smell another and know its history, its territory." On meeting him in a cafe Baumgartner's past reality becomes a problem of "here and now." The young man is blond and bronzed, a propaganda poster of Goebbels's "Aryan Youth." The cafe owner Farrokh does not mention that the man is a German, he just says that he is a foreigner. But Baumgartner knows: "No one had mentioned Germany and had not needed to; one German could tell another always. In the [concentration] camp, they had looked at each other covertly, and not all was German-ness stamped like a number on each, but further information as well—that one was a Jew, another an Aryan. The looks they had exchanged had been the blades of knives slid quickly and quietly between the ribs, with the silence of guilt." He is afraid of the young man. It is an inherent Jewish reflex, inbred through a thousand years of subservience, to kiss the feet that kick you. He believes that this young man has come to get him, and in his mind's eye he is wearing the lederhosen and marching boots of the Hitler Youth. "The campfire and the beer. The beer and the yodelling. The yodelling and the marching. The marching and the shooting. The shooting and the killing. The killing and the killing and the killing." Baumgartner lives in fear of this fair-haired youth right through the story. He feels that he cannot escape the long arm of the dreaded SS. The Third Reich has crumbled into dust many decades ago, but for him, it is there, because all these years in India, he lived that life, and not in the environment of his Indian surrounding. Baumgartner's problem, as that of other refugees, was that they alienated themselves from the present because they were unable to shake off the past. Finally, the young man murders Baumgartner, not because he was a Jew, but for the mundane: money. Throughout the novel the blond German remains a caricature, a creation of Baumgartner's past, but living image of Germany and the blond youths of Hitler's SS. And so in Baumgartner's mind the Nazis do get him after all. Anita Desai also describes the negative attitude of the British to the Jew. The colonial masters are at war with Germany because of Hitler, but even then the Jew stands on a lower rung of the ladder than an Aryan.

Post-war German literature abounds with the Nazi era, but in India it is new. Anita Desai has dug up a past which has been ignored, because the Indians and the English have been fully immersed in their co-relationships. And in this novel, Desai has given expatriates another meaning: that of a refugee from outside the Commonwealth and Empire. I use the word "outside" with intention because the plight of people hounded from their homes has been aptly portrayed in Khushwant Singh's *Train to Pakistan*, Balwant Singh Anand's *Cruel Interlude* and of course, Chaman Nahal's *Gandhi Quartet*.

I doubt what I've been saying has not been without contradictions, for the expatriate, whichever way you look at him or her, as an author or as a character in a novel, is complex, and I am definitely no expert. And though I have been an expatriate for more than half my life in Germany, I can give no cut and dry results. I certainly hope that at this Commonwealth Conference, I'll be able to find the answers.

Patria, Expatriacy, and the Question of Value

G.K. SUBBARAYUDU

To view patria and expatriacy as a pair of words in binary opposition may appear etymologically native. In cognitive terms, however, such a view seems not entirely unsupportable. If it is admitted that patria exerts a powerful and inexorable influence, and that expatriacy is a condition that will be overpowered by this inexorable force, then the basic antagonistic relationship stands cognitively established. The experiential evidence, and the consequent valuative assessment of expatriacy will follow almost as a corollary. The trick is first to see that synergy is only notional and that antagonism is the distinctive feature of this formally united pair of words in which the prefix is semantically only a distancing device but figuratively an instrument of re-cognition.

If, then, patria is primary, what should the value of expatriacy be? Once the valuative framework of expatriacy is established, the value of expatriate experience and literature may be determined.

Since all significant human activity derives from the condition of struggle with the generative environment, the extent and intensity of the condition tends to define the value of such activity. Value, being conditional and not inherent, is capable therefore of mutation with change of condition. Should the condition of struggle be subject to real or notional redefinition, a theoretical stage can emerge, at which it is distinctly possible for struggle to cease, and value of the condition annihilated.

Expatriacy, drawing its value as a metaphor of human struggle, must be reassessed for value because an element of functionality adheres to it vis-a-vis the concept of patria. Expatriacy flows from an original, changeless patria, and seems inevitably to lead back to patria as the sole determinant of perception and value. Therefore the value of expatriacy lies in its strategic significance as opposed to the deterministic significance of patria. Thus, expatriacy is an allegory of the condition of patria, and enables the expatriate to grasp the patria through the allegorization. An expatriate willy-nilly employs expatriacy as a strategy for recovering the patria; so, like all strategies, expatriacy is temporary by nature i.e., role-specific and without value outside the functional scope.

Expatriate experience in literature, then, is to be valued in reference to patria as the desideratum, and not uniquely for itself. Whatever be the emigre's new state, the expatriate is never in a harmonious state till recovery of the patria takes place either in real terms or in notional-historical terms.

Such a critique of expatriacy is well-supported by the experience of the Indian and the West-Indian expatriates, especially as evidenced in some of the fiction that has emerged from these lands. Expatriacy in the colonial/post-colonial phase has an especial poignancy about it, since value often is chimerical (illusionary) in prospect (roads of London paved with gold; London, a new *home* for Mr. Srinivas; Dimple and Amit Basu 'making' a home in America), and negative in retrospect studied with the imminent loss of patria altogether. Kamala Markandaya's *The Nowhere Man*[1] provides the basic emotional substruct of the expatriate experience, where expatriacy loses even its strategic significance; and the loss, juxtaposed with the irrecoverability of patria, renders expatriacy into a caricature instead even of an allegory. Unless pathos is valued aesthetically above its real, human vario, such an expatriate experience can only be perceived as an extension of the colonially imposed alienation, an endless deference of patria, and hence a disjunctor/disruptor of human value.

Mr. Srinivas in Markandaya's novel is an embodiment of this sense of radical disjunction. London is the place (the system) that stands as an allegory of the patria (India). However, even as he moves over this topos, Mr. Srinivas is losing contact with his patria, through his wife's death, son's alienation, and the relationship with old Mrs. Pickering. Srinivas's death in England means that patria can now never be recovered, and that the more the expatriate country establishes its hold over the expatriate, the less its strategic value becomes, dwindling to a point where its value is annihilated. Srinivas's nihilism regarding the failing god of patria while he is in India, leads, in his expatriate state, to annihilation.

I speak of caricature instead of an allegory because, in the allegorical state there is value in expatriacy since it is a reenactment (in a sense) of the value embodied in the patria; but a caricature is mere bold strokes without the ability to hold any content – thus, expatriacy in its annihilative state, having lost all ability to relate to patria, becomes but a caricature.

Again, in Bharati Mukherjee's *Wife,*[2] Dimple Basu, living through the disorienting nightmare of expatriacy, also enters the annihilative state. The rupture with patria occurs in the relationship with Milt Glasser, and must inevitably lead to Amit Basu's annihilation. Had the novel continued, one might even be permitted to wonder whether the action might not have turned self-destructive/annihilative. Does rupture in the expatriate state lead from the self-generative (sui-generis) in the patria to the self-destructive (sui-cida)? Such a possibility seems to lead towards diminution of value. Only so long as the expatriate state enables the protagonist to recover patria, either in real terms or in emotional-notional terms, i.e., it leads back to a real home-country, or a historical tradition, can it lay claim to value.

In Arun Joshi's *The Foreigner*[3] precisely this happens when Sindi Oberoi finally strikes roots in India after the rootless existence in Africa (childhood), England (youth), America (employed state). Babu Rao Khemka, with his talk of an alluring Mussoorie, his homesickness and loneliness, always strikes in Oberoi the one note that must lead him back to patria from his expatriate state. The value of his expatriate experience lies in his final return to India where his interior self finds anchoring space in traditional thought. Otherwise the loneliness he feels, along with Babu Khemka, Srinivas and Dimple Basu should lead from the isolate into the annihilative state.

Everytime a George Lamming protagonist hears a Robeson song in America and thinks of a pan-African or a new black-Caribbean identity; when a Samuel Selvon protagonist in London thinks of his identity in his West Indian homeland with nostalgia, the expatriate country's value rises in proportion. *In the Castle of My Skin*[4] is an excellent case in point. The novel opens with the little boy's words: "Google . . . google . . . no more . . ." which signifies the impatience of a juvescent West Indian with his oppressive environment and lack of identity (cf. George Herbert, "The Collar": I struck the board and cry'd/No more). The phonetic echoes of "Let my people go" – Paul Robeson's song which a grown up Trumper hears in America – which more or less closes the novel, signify the mature recognition of "my people," an identity in the home country. The explosive power of an anthem of black unity is contained in germinal form in the opening words, and serves to underscore the sudden impact of the discovery of an identity as well as the recovery of patria as value from the springboard, as it were, of the expatriate stage.

Thus, it appears that expatriacy tends to be tool in aid of awareness and recovery of patria, and that its value must be defined in relation to patria. Patria seems to be an inescapable power, and expatriacy an indeterminate state whose value fluctuates according to the function it discharges or fulfills.

NOTES

1. Kamala Markandaya, *The Nowhere Man* (Bombay: Sangam Books, 1975).
2. Bharati Mukherjee, *Wife* (New Delhi: Sterling, 1976).
3. Arun Joshi, *The Foreigner* (Bombay: Asia, 1968).
4. George Lamming, *In the Castle of My Skin* (London: Longman, 1970).

The Image of America in Vikram Seth's *The Golden Gate*

Z.N. PATIL

Some literary critics would like to classify Vikram Seth's *The Golden Gate*, a novel that breaks new ground in the sense that it is a novel written in the sonnet form, as an Indian novel in English for the simple reason that Seth, who is now thirty three, was born in Calcutta and lived in India for about the first fifteen years of his life and did not set foot in the United States until he was twenty three. But I personally feel that this alone is not enough to justify the novel as an Indo-English novel. Quite a few critics describe it as a Californian novel. Leslie quotes critics who describe it as "the Great Californian novel" and "a thoroughly Californian novel, peopled by unmistakably Californian characters."[1] Hill comments: "Judging by his novel *The Golden Gate*, it is hard to see how Vikram Seth can be considered an Indian writer, except by accident of birth. There are a few Indian references in the text, such as the 'Taste of Honey' and the charioteer metaphor, and the non-violent attitude of the peace marchers has obvious Gandhian connections . . . but there is nothing here that California has not possessed for a long time. . . . This is, in fact, a totally Californian novel."[2] This is because of Seth's total involvement with life in California. Seth emphasizes that it was not his detachment but rather his love of California that was most valuable to him in writing the novel. Leslie quotes Seth who says, "One can't come with a cold and objective eye from outside and then write with affection about a place. One must have lived years in that place and not just observed for years."[3] The novel is filled with details about California. Even the language of the novel is not Indian English. Peeradina says that he finds hardly any traces of Indianisms in Seth's polished verse, whose idiom is transparently American and more immediately Californian.[4] Thus both linguistically and thematically the novel can be called an American novel.

This brings us to the consideration of the themes in *The Golden Gate*. Before getting down to work, a brief statement of the themes of this novel is needed. We shall find that in the final analysis the themes of the novel can be reduced to three metathemes: (i) the innermost, personal world of men, (ii) man in his activities and relationships with other people, and (iii) man and society, or broader still, man and the surrounding world; but for my convenience, I have classified the themes of this novel as (a) alienation in modern American Society, (b) nuclear insanity, (c) homosexuality, (d) the image of American woman, and (e) disintegration of family life in America.

Trilling comments, "Today, if we are to believe our fiction, the individual is not only isolated from society, he is isolated from everyone he knows, even his own love partner. The connection between people . . . breaks . . . and man lives alone in marriage, in friendship, in nonbusiness, in business."[5] Trilling further adds, "Certainly the striking currency of words like 'isolation' and 'affectlessness' in present day psychiatric studies suggests a new prevalence of the symptoms these words describe."[6] The central figure of *The Golden Gate*, John, with whom the novel begins and ends, is an isolated, lonely person. He is a blond-haired, good-looking, healthy, employed, ambitious, sound, solvent, self-made, self-possessed but depressed person. He is a young man of twenty six and is described as aloof, prim and lonely. He craves for a family that will cushion his solitude. His life has grown duller since he left college. Throughout the novel John Brown, who is engaged in constant change of partners, the changing relationship being almost similar to the game of musical chairs, undergoes tantalizing amorous experiences. Initially he is seen as caught in the kelp of loneliness – a lonely and dispirited man with irregular, moronic sentimentality due to his being a linkless node having no spouse or sibling and children. He then is confronted with two eccentric candidates for marriage: Wasp Bluestocking and Belinda Beale, but unfortunately for him the former turns out to be an intellectual bore like Henrietta in Susan Gaskell's *Suppressed Desires* and the latter nauseatingly physical in her first encounter with him. After having been disillusioned in his adventures with the two ladies who responded to his personal matrimonial ad, John whose cookie also asks him to forget the entanglement of love, hopefully turns to find his love partner in

Elisabeth Dorati, a young urban professional, an attorney working in a law firm. But the unfortunate part of it is that she deserts him and marries Philip Weiss instead. This aggravates his feeling of loneliness and gives him a sense of injured pride and renders him more loveless and his life more pain-aversive than before he met Liz. Naturally enough he diverts his attention to Janet Hayakawa, John's former beloved who is saddened by the way John's friendships have all gone astray; but she is too busy and her artistic life too hurried for more than sympathy. The final blow comes when Janet dies in an accident and John is left totally alone. Thus Janet's death completes the process of John's isolation. Phil tells Liz: "The fact is, he's so isolated/By all his pain and bitterness./There's not much we can do, I guess."[7] (13.43) Thus John is lonely, isolated, alienated and lost, sans love, and sans lover at the beginning and so is he at the close of the novel. Emptiness leads to nothing but emptiness.

There are people like John who fail even in their pursuit of female love; but there are people like Philip who succeed on both the male and the female fronts. Phil, who was once married to Claire, enjoys both the original and the alternative services. Ed, a man with a sissyfied appearance, gives him passionate company not only in conversation but in his bed. Their relationship is born out of need and infatuation. John holds anti-homosexual opinions thinking that gay life is irreconcilable to family life. He seems to subscribe to the view that male and female are programmed to mate with the opposite sex. That is why he is greatly surprised and disgusted with Phil and exclaims: "Oh, Jesus, Phil, but you were married. . . . Oh, Jesus, Phil – what do you find/In – what do two men do together?" (9.15) But Phil is not like John who believes in hetero-sexuality; nor does he share Vittorio's view in Andrew Holleran's novel *Nights in Aruba* who believes, "You can have boys like that, or you can have the pleasures of family life. But you can't have both." (107) Phil does not agree to the view that gay and family life are mutually exclusive or that one is the enemy of the other. For him homosexuality and hetero-sexuality are not substitutes but are complementary to each other. Phil had homosexual relations with a guy at college and he would acknowledge, even when married, now and then, his eye might stray toward other men. This becomes clear through Phil's discourses which are attempts not only to justify but even glorify homosexuality. He breaks out of the totemic world of his ancestors and enters the rational world of science where sexual expression is freed from religious taboos. He has never bothered with convention. Seth describes at length their nights spent together, their magnetic draw of each other, their physical encounters, their caresses and their love-making. Phil and Ed are erotically attracted and at some points sound like man and woman or lover and beloved. Indeed, these scenes are a mockery and a devastating parody of heterosexual love. It is ironic that Seth describes the Phil-Ed affair in almost as romantic a fashion as he does the John-Liz affair.

There are several attempts on the part of Phil and Ed respectively to glorify and condemn homosexuality. The former, who is a hedonist and a sceptic, furnishes justifications of the alternative service on logical and practical grounds whereas the latter condemns it in biblical terms. Phil maintains that the outmoded biblical rules need no longer be adhered to or believed in. He argues that God will not mind their physical touches, their caresses and sighs because, as he says, earthly, bodily beauty does not exist just for contemplation. He defends his acts by saying that God has created his perfect physical form, his lovely body, with a definite purpose of making their lives warm. He continues: "You have a mind too, Ed. Why don't you go by what your heart says is right. . . . Do you remember our first night? Do you remember it? Why won't you defer to strong love instead of spectral voices in your head?" (8.33) He further adds, "When your heart's aching with desire, should something that you've somewhere read by someone two millennia dead convince you that your heart's a liar?" (8.34) Phil asks Ed not to play the game by other's rules. Finally Phil, an indefatigable commentator on the topic, voices his monistic or holistic approach to the object of his sex when he says, "Love is whole or else it's nothing. I can't see you Ed, as this disembodied soul." (8.35) Phil's admonitions remind us of the courtly love tradition where the lover pursues his lady with constant appeals and pesterings.

Ed's reference point of anti-homosexual opinions is 'religion' or 'sin' or the scriptures. He expresses, with puritanical purity, his own contempt for their love-making. He wants to keep their spirits warm through the shared touch of conversation. But his censorious conscience is dormant during nights and during daytime he considers homosexuality both as a disease and a sin. It is not the fear of social condemnation and judicial punishment but of religious contamination. But the irony is that Ed's religion does not square too well with his lust. His homosexual adventures are followed by his confessions in the church which ease the pricking of his relentless conscience. He feels a deep Catholic guilt about his sexuality—a guilt which drives him into sexual activities and then delivers him into long periods of sexual renunciation. As Phil suggests, this guilt Ed feels has been imposed on him from without, that in his guilt and self-loathing he is only following a text written by someone else and taught by conventional morality. Ed argues that he has to trust the decisions of his faith and not batten on his own volitions. He takes recourse to the Bible which says that if a man lies with a man, he is bound to die. He treats his body as divine instrument and his love for Phil as platonic. He says, "I love you Phil, but my desire goes beyond sex. Lovers indeed must shed more than their clothes. They need to shed their bodies. Flesh and fire can meet but can't merge. It's a state only our souls can consummate. If lovers cannot cease caressing, isn't it that they long to find their bodies' unity expressing a truer unison of mind?" (8.19-20) Thus one day Phil and Ed are lovers, and the next day Phil is gagged with sacramental text. Gradually the affair goes defunct. The end of this homosexual relationship is stated in Phil's own words: "I loved a woman and was dropped—/I loved a man—and that also flopped." (11.20)

The Phil-Ed affair is representative of the prevalence of homosexuality in California, especially in San Francisco. Towne discusses the prevalence of this way of life in America.[8] Meyers talks of homosexuality as one important theme in modern literature.[9] In the modern period homosexuals have become an important literary subject, giving rise to gay literature. Vikram Seth's novel might be classified as a gay work because a large part of it is devoted to the Phil-Ed affair. Ironically enough, Phil, a homosexual, is rewarded with Elisabeth and later on is shown jubilant over the addition of a new member to his family: his household greets its latest member with vast jocosity and joy; on the contrary, the novel begins with John as a lonely, depressed and dispirited man walking across the Golden Gate Park and ends with him depleted by his pain on the loss of his beloved. There is no one to console him except the imaginary voice of Janet who is no more.

Seth has succeeded in wielding his poetry in every direction—description, narration, dialogues and even sermonic lectures on nuclear madness and appeal for nuclear disarmament, which is one of the themes of the novel. Philip, a friend of John, worked in the Lungless Labs—a place which breeds bombs; but he gave up his job because it troubled his conscience to work in a bomb-making factory. He does not want the world to be exploded with playloads and blow-guns. He argues that the explosions of bombs will cause ecological imbalance and horrible irremediable diseases affecting not only the human world but also the animal and the vegetable world. The demonstrators who carry placards which read "I am my brother's keeper," "Nice Folks don't use nukes," "Work for life, not death" (7.9) includes Charlemagne, the anti-nuclear cat of Elisabeth with her typical placard that reads: "Cats and attorneys are disarming. Why aren't we all?" Elisabeth also gives an anti-nuclear talk before the demonstrators protesting against the crazy ways of the world. She expresses her fear about the possible nuclear killing of all the other fauna. Father O'Hare expresses his concern about the liquidation mankind is racing to. He believes in the equation that killing is dying. He talks of the massive machine that may cause mutual extermination, common death or omnicide. He indefatigably sermonizes on nuclear insanity and hate citing historical references and examples of war. His argument that there is no victory, no survival, no defense, no place to hide in this exhaustive fratricide that threatens all culture and all civilization, all human kind and all creation, resembles, on the face of it, the argument put forth by President Reagan: "A nuclear war cannot be won and must never be fought"—words that the President and General Secretary Gorbachev agreed on in their joint statement at Geneva a year ago. The solution suggested by the demonstrators is that of non-violent and peaceful co-existence.

It is significant that women, like Elisabeth who is a young attorney in Cobb and Kearny law firm, participate in the anti-nuclear demonstration. She represents American women pacifists. She is one of those American women who have emancipated and saved themselves from being the dreary, depressed housewives trapped in lifeless housework and who have either discovered their strength or are in the process of discovering it. Elisabeth Dorati is a strong egalitarian woman able to control her destiny. She, as a peace marcher, argues that our nuclear insanity will result in starvation, blindness, reduction of ozone due to overload of nitrogen oxides, horrible increase in ultraviolet rays and finally universal annihilation. Elisabeth is not the only woman participating in the peace movement—Rowena Craven is another lady who is a pacifist.

The American woman is equally successful in artistic field. Sue Dorati is a marvellous musician and Janet Hayakawa is a drummer in a band called Liquid Sheep. Moreover, she is a sculptor waiting for sober critical attention which her Three Eggs, An Adolescent Lion, Clothed Nude, Study of Young Man Caught in Eagles Claws, Ma Hen and Biased Portrait of an Ogress have not yet brought her. Nevertheless, in spite of malicious critical efforts during her lifetime to label her works as "feeble" and as inferior to the works of Moore and Calder in terms of inspiration and artistic versatility, her sculptural models are posthumously acclaimed as "classics" displaying "strength," "sureness and maturity" and she is ranked with great sculptors like Moore, Kurosawa, Pollock, Ashley and Cage. Thus Vikram Seth has successfully presented to us a portrait of young American woman as artist.

Another aspect of the American woman's personality is her fondness for cats and iguanas. Elisabeth Dorati, daughter of Mike Dorati and Marie Dorati, represents the class of cat freaks. Though she is a dynamite in bed, John is unhappy with her because of her exhibitionistic extravagant compulsions and her obsessive, excessive love of Charlemagne, her anti-nuclear cat. Another character who is very much fond of cats is Janet Hayakawa who feeds her "Egyptian Deities" called Cuff and Link on fish and cream and gives them love and indulgence. The fact that these cats have silken beds and baskets woven with golden letters speaks volumes for Janet's craze for cats.

Though the American woman is playing different roles in her society, her key roles are in her family: woman as wife and mother. It is in order to acquire these significant roles that Wasp Bluestocking and Belinda Beale respond to John Brown's personal, matrimonial advertisement. But both of them fail in their attempts to trap John who is in search of love and company that will breach his fearsome solitude. Out of a pile of pornographic replies to his advertisement, he selects these two, desperately hoping to get a suitable love partner. He takes Wasp to see *Macbeth* where he is bored by her insistent exegesis. The literary critic in her overtakes her amorous self. She untiringly talks of appearance and reality themes, the significance of dreams and darkness, and the singular thesis that the Third Murderer is the central figure of each act. Throughout the meal she oozes French and throughout the play she oozes critical jargon. Thus her philosophizing renders John pale and white as Banquo's ghost.

Belinda Beale is the second candidate contesting the selection. Unfortunately for John, she is another imbalanced and partial woman. In her, the physical is dominant over the intellectual. She is a pornographic maenad mad with morbid lust. She is highly sex-conscious, sex-obsessed, almost sex-mad. Her passionate petrissage during the play shocks John and her disgusting physical movements underneath the dining table horrify and render him mute. These two ladies might be described as perverted counterparts of D.H. Lawrence's Miriam and Clara in *Sons and Lovers.*

Families do not loom large in Seth's novel. It is the young unmarried ladies who play the decisive roles. Nevertheless, old ladies do play certain roles in the novel. Mrs. Marie Dorati, wife of Mike Dorati and mother of Elisabeth, Edward and Sue, is a loving and anxious mother. This rheumatic lady fears that her children might prove a fruitless crew and she might die a grandchildless death. Fortunately, she lives to see Elisabeth's married love, her ripening years and the boon of a child. She goes rapturous about her grandson and like any other grandmother gloats over the nose and smiles of the child: "Look that nose, Mike – it recaptures my father's nose. Look, look, he smiled. Oh, what a darling – what a beauty – what name have you decided on?" (13.48)

We also get a glimpse of the disintegrating family system in America. We do not come across the ideal, gentle and good woman – loved, loving, unselfish, self-sacrificing wife and mother and the eternal virgin. Seth has given us a realistic portrayal of American women who seem to be deficient in love, tenderness or even in any feminine fullness. Women in *The Golden Gate* do not seem to act as full individuals. Moreover, the increasing "emancipation" of women has done nothing to ease the situation, but rather tends to exacerbate it. The love-life of husband and wife is not satisfactory and they are mutually incompatible and ill-adjusted. Claire, after having lived with Phil for six years, leaves him on the pretext of Phil's domineering disposition. Though a year has passed since her departure, she neither visited nor phoned nor sent a gift to her six-year-old son Paul. The reason she gives for her not visiting her son is that her erratic visits might create anxiety in Paul. Phil married in haste and now repents at leisure. In fact, they were happy, had a son, invested in a piano, plenty of furniture, a Ford Capri, Insurance, dishwasher, and television. Their home was what Phil had always longed and prayed for. But today Phil's divorce from Claire has left Paul craving for a mother who once kissed him and read him stories in bed. Paul's question to his father in the following conversation is a sardonic comment on the state the family system in America is reduced to:

> "No Paul, she's gone away."
> "Forever?"
> "I just can't tell you, son—but never think you're alone. You've got me."
> "When will you leave me?" Phil, shocked, stares. (3.19)

In conclusion, it can be said that the individual in America today feels isolated in spite of God's plenty around him. As far as human relations are concerned, the social atmosphere of the United States, as Dingwall comments, "is . . . not particularly conducive to purity of thought or deed."[10] This observation is confirmed when fictional personalities like Phil talk about gay bars in San Francisco where people paw on handsome young nice guys. So is the case with the American women. All is not well with the American woman. Now before coming to the close of the paper, a word of caution is needed. I have tried to avoid generalizations and when the words 'American woman' are used, no suggestion is to be entertained that I mean every American woman.

NOTES

1. Jacques Leslie, "Rhyme and Reason," *Span* (Nov. 1986), p. 4.
2. Rowena Hill, "Vikram Seth's *The Goldern Gate*: A Quick Look," *The Literary Criterion*, vol. XXI, no. 4 (1986), p. 87.
3. Leslie, p. 4.
4. Saleem Piradeena, "A Californian Ballad," *The Indian Express*, Magazine Section, 10 August 1986.
5. Diana Trilling, "The Image of Women in Contemporary Literature," in R.J. Lifton, ed., *The Woman in America* (Boston: Houghton, Mifflin, 1965), p. 61.
6. *Ibid.*, p. 68.
7. Vikram Seth, *The Golden Gate* (Delhi: OUP, 1986).
8. A. Towne, "Homosexuality in American Culture," *American Mercury* (August 1951), LXXIII, pp. 3-9 and LXXIV, pp. 22-27.
9. Jeffrey Meyers, *Homosexuality and Literature: 1890-1930* (Univ. of London: The Athlone Press, 1977), p. 1.
10. E.J. Dingwall, *The American Woman, A Historical Study* (London: Gerald Druckworth, 1956), p. 201.

Of Living in Two Cultures: Expatriate Women in Jhabvala's Fiction

A. HARI PRASANNA

> The advantange (or disadvantage) of living in two cultures strikes one at every turn.[1]

Indian writing in English owes much to the historical phenomenon of juxtaposition of the two diametrically opposite cultures, namely the oriental and the occidental. It is not unnatural that the Indo-English writers should dwell on the cultural and psychological upheavals and the reactions and responses that emerge as the result of the East-West encounter.

Besides, there are writers "who could neither inhabit the country nor reject it but continued to be nostalgic about it in their literatures from abroad."[2] Ruth Prawer Jhabvala, one of the better known women novelists of India, belongs to this category of fiction-writers.

Jhabvala can be described as an 'inside-outsider' as well as an 'outside-insider.' These terms impinge upon her personal and literary situation. From the European point of view she may seem an 'outside-insider' while from Indian artistic viewpoint she appears an 'inside-outsider.' She is essentially a European writer who has lived in India and given to her experience of life and society in this country an artistic expression.[3]

Jhabvala came to India at the age of 24 as the bride of a young Parsi architect. Her creative urge found its artistic expression during her twenty-four years' stay in India. She has written eight novels and a number of short stories. Her work shows that India is her preoccupation. Again and Again she turns to the theme of interaction between the two cultures, namely European and Indian. She has explored "the themes of expatriates in India and the mixed marriage of Indian and European."[4] She minutely studies the impact of India on European expatriates. Her preoccupation with India confers on her a distinguished position in the world of Indian-English literature. Though she rejects labels she states categorically that she is essentially a European writer: "I have lived in India for most of my adult life. My husband is Indian and so are my children. I am not, and less so every year."[5]

Whatever Jhabvala's relationship with India and Europe may be, as far as her fiction is concerned, India seems to be her theme as well as obsession. Her awareness of various aspects of Indian life establishes the Indianness of her fiction. Her close personal experience of Indian life and her exclusive interest in it as a novelist as well as her ability to identify very closely with Indians, notably with Indian women, take her nearer to native writers like R.K. Narayan and Raja Rao.[6] As Vasant A. Shahane says her creative work provides ample evidence of her Indianness.[7] She gives us in her fiction the experience of European women married to Indians or of Indian women married to Europeans who are confronted with the inevitable situation of the Hindu joint families.[8]

As a woman writer with her sensitve perception of the human relationship Jhabvala handles the situations from the perspective of the relationship between man and woman – in and out of marriage – which naturally is most intimate and hence most complex. The problems of the expatriates, their psychological turmoil and cultural schizophrenia are dealt with insight and understanding.

Jhabvala speaks of the emotional stages every European living in India undergoes. She says "first stage, tremendous enthusiasm – everything Indian is marvellous; second stage, everything Indian not so very marvellous; third stage, everything Indian abominable."[9]

Judy of *A Backward Place* is an exception to this emotional upheaval. She does not dislike India or Indian way of life. She marries an Indian for love, and she sticks to him in spite of the testing times they have. Judy tries her level best and almost suceeds in adapting herself to Indian ways of life. Her positive attitude to life helps her accept the challenges of life. Her readiness to identify herself with the lower middle class Indian family in which she lives gives her a sense of belonging and saves her from the theme of cultural alienation. One can see that "the marriage of Bal and Judy is difficult not because of the difference in race so much as because of the clash in their temperaments between the dreamer and the pragmatist."[10] She retains her English pragmatism and Anglo-Saxon coolness, but these very qualities, instead of working as barriers in her coming closer to her people, help her put up with Bal's childish irresponsibility and impractical optimism.

Judy can be happy because she is neither like Etta, who hates and despises India, yet is imprisoned there, nor Clarissa who is a victim of self-deception in her profound love for India. She retained her English qualities like imperturbability and cool composure while adapting Indian ways of life and dressing. Judy is happy in her home which has not even a sofa because she finds it just the opposite of the house she lived in as a girl with her parents: "The light little home with the doors and curtains firmly shut to keep the cold and strangers out."[11] She enjoyed the open life in India and finds in her home "a refuge from loneliness, insularity to the psychological disintegration that has overtaken her mother in Britain."[12]

Judy is cautious, hard-working and realistic to the core. Her too much of pragmatism is in a way balanced by Bal's impracticable dreams. She saves for future yet loves to listen to Bal's hopes and ambitions. She insists on Bal's attending to their sick son, refuses to invest on his unfounded dreams, rejects his idea of all. Her maturity of mind and balanced behaviour check Bal's childish and unsteady attitude. She sticks to her decision to work in spite of Bal's protests and theatrical outbursts. She loves him so much that she likes him even when she is quarrelling with him. (222-23)

Judy is so firm and self-willed that all the attempts of Etta to make her regret her marriage with Bal prove futile. She admires Etta's very English room, her dresses and sophistication but does not allow them to influence her or depress her. Clarissa praises her that she "had the good sense to realize that the only way to live here was to turn herself into a real Indian wife." (25) Her adaptability to and identification with the country she chooses to live in, her realistic attitude and contentment stand her in good stead. Vasant A. Shahane finds Judy "the finest embodiment of this identification" and sees her "to be truly an Indian wife."[13]

After much deliberation Judy finally agrees to go to Bombay with Bal, leaving behind the security of her job and income. Her first reaction to Bal's suggestion that they should all go to Bombay, however, was rebellion. Her English self sprang to the surface. She "felt herself so very adult and sensible and very English. English people did not behave like that, the moment give up everything they had and go wandering off in search of no one know what." (219) Bhanji's religious faith and spiritual peace provided her with an answer to her fears and doubts regarding their future. So she accepts to face the challenge by consoling herself that she can find a job in Bombay though "it would mean going around . . . and wait about in people's offices and be told 'no' many times over, but even that would not be so bad. She had done it before, she could do it again." (223)

In the light of this study Connie Hayball's pronouncement that "Judy, the most attractive of Europeans is a passive character"[14] does not hold good. Judy has the courage to accept, which should not be taken to be passivity. It is Judy's love for Bal and her readiness to adapt and accept, that help her to be happy and contented in the face of adversity and want too. H.M. Williams sees her to be "the very embodiment of commonsense of Anglo-Saxon coolness."[15] These are the very qualities that make her bring harmony into her married life. Judy is Ruth Prawer Jhabvala's positive and affirmative answer to the doubts and fears that surround an inter-racial, inter-religious marriage.

There is no problem with characters like Judy in Jhabvala's *A Backward Place*, who accept India and adjust to it. But Etta and Clarissa in the same novel find it difficult to cope with India. Etta, a middle-aged Hungarian woman, has come to India as a result of her marriage to an Indian student. The marriage has proved to be a failure and Etta has had a number of love-affairs after that. Her present affair is with a rich hotel owner, Mr. Gupta. Etta is conscious of her waning beauty and is at pains to retain the love of her recent lover. The rapid changes that age bring on her, coupled with her fear that she is losing hold on Gupta, make Etta feel desperate. She is unhappy because she tries to resist India instead of being absorbed by it. She despises the country, describes it as a primitive society with primitive morality. She feels that "the Indian sun has been put specially into the sky to ruin our complexions." (7) Trapped and imprisoned in a country which she hates, Etta becomes depressed and even hysterical at the thought of isolation and loneliness awaiting her. It is true that "Jhabvala treats Etta with sympathy mixed characteristically some irony aimed at her pretentiousness."[16]

Clarissa unlike Etta has come to India inspired by the works of Vivekananda and Romain Rolland. She describes herself as a spiritual seeker and says that she is in India out of conviction and idealism. In spite of her professed love for India and her sympathy for its poor, she is in perpetual quest for a comfortable life. Etta is at least definite about her dislike for India, but Clarissa is not sure of her reaction and responses. She professes love for India, wears sarees, praises Judy for attempting to be an Indian wife, appreciates her house because it has character, but hesitates to use their rather primitive bathroom. She pretends to be too busy chasing the eternal values to care for worldly matters. Yet she lives comfortably on the hospitality of her rich friends. Though she claims to be as free as a bird, she is a prisoner to her own delusions about India.

Clarissa is unable to come to terms with the real India, for, it has nothing to do with the idealized picture of India she has created in her imagination after reading the books by Vivekananda and Romain Rolland. She is a victim of self-deception when she speaks of the sort of vibration between these people of India and herself while the reality is that she is chased by urchins and pestered by beggars with whom she loses temper unashamedly. Thus there is something pathetic about Clarissa.

Etta unlike Clarissa tries to create a little Europe in her room, but it is a cage – "a cage that was necessary to her and out of which she would not break even if she could." (212) It seems that "Jhabvala now develops her description of her characters' homes to indicate their relationship with the country – for the Europeans they are places of refuge, little bits of Europe."[17] Etta considers herself a prisoner in India, not a guest. Though Jhabvala's handling of Etta is ironic, it is not lacking in sympathy. Etta clings desperately to Gupta while he tries to disengage himself. Yet she convinces herself that "it was not for him she was doing it. It was the trip abroad. She was handling him, she was being clever." (147)

When all her efforts to win Gupta fail, Etta's attempts at suicide have a touch of theatricality. After taking a few pills she telephones Hochstadts. They did not panic for they were shrewd enough to know that Etta had not taken very many pills. Probably she had intended, at least and pretended herself that she intended to finish the bottle, but by the time she had swallowed a not too many fearful number, she had thought of the Hochstadts and had picked up the telephone. It was not unlikely that she had bethought herself of the swallowing and the only factor she had been imprecise about just exactly at what stage to call them. (226) Thus Jhabvala treats the pretentiousness of Etta with ironic amusement as a result of which Etta evokes sympathy rather than disgust.

The more Etta hates the country, the harder it becomes for her to live there. As Margaret Berry observes, "Etta is simply condemned to fade away after an attempted suicide – blaming as she disappears not her own unwise and fevered choices, but the backward place that is India."[18]

Clarissa relentlessly pursues Etta, if only to make herself comfortable. H.M. Williams feels that "her relationship with Etta has the stormy quality of a love affair."[19] Clarissa is poor and has none else to turn to and that is why she clings to Etta. But behind her back Clarissa does not hesitate to pass disparaging remarks against Etta. Both Etta and Clarissa are trapped in India and are condemned to live there. Etta continues to nourish her hatred for the backward place. Clarissa has come to India chasing the spirituality as she conceived it from Romain Rolland's *Life of Vivekananda*, Edwin Arnold's *Light of Asia* and everyman's edition of the *Gita*.[20]

Olivia of *Heat and Dust*[21] is a complete contrast to Judy of *A Backward Place*. She is a pretty young woman, rather vain, pleasure-seeking and a little petulant. She comes to India with her husband Douglas whom she thinks she loves. But shortly after her arrival in India she meets the Nawab, feels attracted towards him and has an affair with him. Though Olivia succeeds in keeping away the heat and dust of India by shutting all the doors and windows, she succumbs to the heat of passion in herself. She gets her pregnancy aborted for fear that the child would betray her to her husband.

Unlike Olivia, the narrator of *Heat and Dust* has come to India to seek a "simpler and more natural way of life." She "rejects the world of illusion in which her predecessor lived,"[22] adopts Indian way of living and dressing; tries to learn Hindi, wears a saree and is always open and frank in her sexual relationship. She accepts the advances of Chid because she is more liberal-minded and modern than Olivia in matters of sex. She decides to have the child by Inder instead of aborting it like Olivia. But whereas Olivia stays in India out of necessity the narrator does so out of her choice – because she is dissatisfied with the western values and looks towards a simple but meaningful life in India.

Olivia refuses to take a decision unless everything becomes known. The narrator on the other hand being frank and courageous is never at any doubt as to what she should do. She chooses to live all alone on the isolated hills whereas Olivia is forced to do so.

The narrator "belongs to a new generation of liberal-minded educated travellers from the West, who consciously strive to communicate with India"[23] and her decision to go up the hills is an effort in understanding spiritual India.

Once again in *A New Dominion* Jhabvala portrays the western women and their attempt to grapple with spiritual India. Three girls Lee, Margaret and Evie come to India in search of spiritual truth and peace. Lee comes to India "to lose herself in order to find herself."[24] She wants to have a pure heart untainted by modern materialism. She comes to India as a revolt against her life at home and her family. Evie has been in India for three years with Swamiji and it is all she wants. The fact is Evie is bound to him in some mysterious way, from which bondage she never tries to be free. While "Lee and Margaret seek a merging of their selves with that of the Swamiji, as a symbol of India's heritage of mysticism and spiritual glory, Evie is even more intensely identified with what she believes to be the soul of India as embodied in the Swamiji."[25]

These three girls who have rejected the European materialistic life have come to India to take refuge and find solace in the Eastern spirituality. Unfortunately they come across a spurious Swamiji. Jhabvala's attitude to the spiritual guides in India is obvious in the presentation of the Swamiji. Her satire, however, is not confined to the worldly materialistic goodness alone. The spiritual seekers from the West are not spared. The West turns to the East, not because it believes, trusts and admires the spirituality of the East, but to fill the vacuum in their lives. One cannot find fault with Jhabvala for the distorted picture of Swamiji, for India has no dearth of such fake Swamis. The irony levelled at such godmen also brings out the hollow nature of the Western spiritual seekers, for, they are most of the time attracted to the life of Swamiji than to genuine ones. They look at Swamiji, as a symbol of India's spirituality and seek complete identification with him. The tragedy is that they do not know what they want, nor do they know where they can find it. They get confused between physical union and spiritual communion. Therefore they submit to the lust of Swamiji.

NOTES

1. Cited by O.P. Bhatnagar in his "Commonwealth Literature: Genesis and Bearings," *Indian Readings in Commonwealth*

Literature (New Delhi: Sterling, 1985), p. 28.
2. *Ibid*., p. 30.
3. Vasant A. Shahane, *Ruth Prawer Jhabvala* (New Delhi: Arnold Heinemann, 1976), p. 24.
4. H.M. Williams, *The Fiction of Ruth Prawer Jhabvala* (Calcutta: Writers Workshop, 1973), p. 10.
5. Quoted by Vasant A. Shahane, p. 24.
6. H.M. Williams, "Stranger in a Backward Place," *The Journal of Commonwealth Literature*, 6 (June 1977), p. 53.
7. Vasant A. Shahane, p. 24.
8. *Ibid*., p. 18.
9. Cited by Yasmine Gooneratne, *Silence, Exile and Cunning: The Fiction of Ruth Prawer Jhabvala* (New Delhi: Orient Longman, 1983), p. 7.
10. H.M. Williams, *The Fiction of Ruth Prawer Jhabvala*, p. 49.
11. Ruth Prawer Jhabvala, *A Backward Place* (New Delhi: Orient, 1965), p. 39.
12. Yasmine Gooneratne, p. 159.
13. Vasant A. Shahane, p. 81.
14. Connic Hayball, "Ruth Prawer Jhabvala's India," *The Journal of Indian Writing in English*, 9, no. 2 (July 1981), p. 49.
15. H.M. Williams, "Strangers in a Backward Place," p. 60.
16. *Ibid*., p. 61.
17. Connic Hayball, p. 48.
18. Margaret Berry, "India A Double Key," *The Journal of Indian Writing in English*, 6, no. 1 (Jan. 1978), p. 52.
19. H.M. Williams, *The Fiction of Ruth Prawer Jhabvala*, p. 52.
20. Margaret Berry, p. 52.
21. *Heat and Dust* (New Delhi: Hind, 1975), p. 99.
22. Margaret P. Joseph, "Cinematic Technique in *Heat and Dust*," *Journal of Literature and Aesthetics*, nos. 2 and 3 (April-July 1982), p. 45.
23. Yasmine Gooneratne, p. 22.
24. *A New Dominion* (London: Granada, 1983), p. 10.
25. Vasant A. Shahane, "Ruth Prawer Jhabvala's New Dominion," *Journal of Commonwealth Literature*, 12, no. 1 (August 1977), p. 48.

Multicultural Ethos in the Fiction of Margaret Laurence and Anita Desai: A Comparative Note

D.K. PABBY

Both Canada and India have been colonies of the British Empire and are now members of the Commonwealth. But one can easily perceive the vast difference between the two different ways which the Europe in general and England in particular had their impact on the social, political, cultural and literary milieu of the two countries. If the immigrant Europeans settled down in the vast land of Canada called the prairies to make it their permanent homeland, India remained subjugated as an exploited and slave nation of the Britishers for more than three hundred years. However, one may surmise that India too can claim European lineage as the Aryans, the first inhabitants of the land, are said to have come from Europe (as European invaders) through the north-western passes as early as 1500 B.C., and then they settled on the banks of the river Indus to create a mighty civilization.

The geo-physical factors in Canada made it an entirely different country from any of the typical European countries the inhabitants of which had migrated to Canada to settle there on permanent basis. But the cultural ethos they brought with them made Canada, culturally and linguistically speaking, 'a healthy mosaic' as against the 'melting pot' culture of America. The Indian position was, however, quite different. India had a glorious cultural heritage that went back to the Vedic era. But the interaction with the western world through the Britishers, the Portuguese and the French for about three hundred years did bring forth some new patterns of cultural behaviour and value-system which generated new tensions in society. Twentieth century Indian writers took due note of these, and the themes and art of characterization in their writings bear ample testimony to it. These writers including Anita Desai articulate important questions in their works regarding tradition versus modernity, dwindling of the conventional value system, marital discords, collapse of the joint family system, lure of getting rich even through questionable means, ambivalent cultural responses to the impact of the West, social and economic disparities, colonial consciousness as a hangover of the British rule etc. But the picture that emerges in the case of Canada is vastly different. The natives there had hardly any literary tradition of their own except in some folk forms. The task of the writers there whose parents had come from European countries, was chiefly confined to articulating the passions, hopes, aspirations and apprehensions of the new emerging nation and to carve out norms for cultural rootedness. Hence, the main thematic concerns perceptible in their works are the question of a distinct identity of their own as different from that of the Europeans and the Americans, prairies and their impact on the lives of the people, the problems and aspirations of the natives, impact of the immigrant cultures, feminism etc.

Thus one common factor, at least at one plane, that emerges here is that of the multicultural or cross-cultural ethos that marks the writings of most of the writers in Canada and India. Margaret Laurence and Anita Desai, two representative novelists of these two countries not only exhibit a distinct and deep awareness of the social, economic and cultural realities around them, but they also succeed in effectively transmuting them into their literary experiences and assimilating the same in their writings. Multiplicity of thematic patterns and poly-angular perspectives in their writings clearly bring forth the multicultural ethos that forms the basis of their writings. An attempt has been made, in this paper, to analyze these themes, character portrayals and the evocative symbolism in two of their major novels viz. *The Diviners* and *Baumgartner's Bombay* so as to reinforce the proposition of multiculturism being one of the predominant aspects of their literary perspectives.

In an essay titled "Ivory Tower or Grassroots?: The Novelist as Socio-Political Being," Margaret Laurence has rightly argued for a view of fiction as 'social commentary' also and has identified several social, cultural and political concerns emerging in her own works. One of these, alongwith those of several other authors as Rudy Wiebe *(The Temptations of the Big Bear)* and Peter Such *(Riverrun)*, is the dispossession and alienation of Canada's native people at more than one levels. In fact, just as Anita Desai's novel *Baumgartner's Bombay* provided her with an opportunity to explore her German background that she had inherited from her mother's side (as a child); Margaret Laurence's last novel in the Manawaka series, *The Diviners*, also gives Laurence a chance to delve deep into her own Scottish-Presbyterian origins and heritage. In her essay titled "A Place to Stand on," she has clearly stated:

> I recognised that in some way not at all consciously understood by me, I had to begin approaching my background and my past through my grand parents' generation, the generation of Scots Presbyterian origin, who had been among the first to people the town I called Manawaka. This was where my roots began. Other past generations of my father's family had lived in Scotland, but for me, my people's real past – my own real past – was not connected except distantly with Scotland.

In fact, both the novelists under reference appear to conclusively arrive at the realization that 'past shapes us as much as we shape our past,' though this may appear to be 'an apparently impossible contradiction' as appears to be the case with the topical sentence with which *The Diviners* opens i.e. 'The river flowed bothways.' As a matter of fact, the protagonist of this novel, Morag Gunn, reflects quite early in the novel like this: "A popular misconception is that we cann't change the past," but she asserts "everyone is constantly changing their own past, recalling it, revisiting it." (60)

The Diviners partially provides an answer to this popular misconception. This gets illustrated from the fact that the past events in the novel are narrated in the present tense and the present events in the past tense. In fact, Laurence offers us double perspective on her protagonist Morag Gunn. We see her from the inside, we share her thoughts and experience her feelings in the 'Memorybank Movies' and 'Snapshots' in the first three parts of the novel where the flashback technique has been innovatively used. And we witness her coming to terms with her life's realities and ironies when we find her in the act of writing, of giving significant shape to those through her books in the last two parts. But along with this, Laurence's use of the third person, compels us to view Morag from the outside as well i.e. from a distance. And we see her life getting shaped by her experiences, not only composing the story of her life but also being composed by it – a product of the pressures working on her mind and being subjected to the patriarchal discourses of her day.

These thematic patterns in the *The Diviners* are articulated through Morag's changing awareness with the other main characters in the novel. Born as she is in a middle-class white family, she does not consider her low-class foster-parents – Christie, the town's garbage-collector and his wife Prin who dresses in a socially awkward and unacceptable manner, as her real parents. In other words, through the loss of her physical parents, she appears to have been deprived of her past inheritance at the social and cultural level. But it is clear that although through his tales of the clan Gunn, her foster father manages to create a half-imaginary world with which the orphan girl may identify herself; yet the agony and suffering of the dispossessed and exploited clans of the highlands (the Metis) and their struggle for survival get evocatively mirrored.

Similarly, through her relationship with Jules Tonnerre, Laurence lays bare the social and cultural alienation of the so-called French half-breeds who have been deprived of the right to assert their identity in the white-dominated society and who have to feel contented with earning their livelihood with singing of the folk songs of their clans. Their pitiable situation gets poignantly depicted through the harsh fact that when Jules Tonnerre's father died, he was denied admittance into the town's cemetery because the people i.e. the white settlers were afraid of 'his half-breed bones spoiling their graveyard.'

The third major relationship of Morag and her English Professor husband Brooke Skelton which ends soon with a divorce, is yet another reminder of the sad situation of the repression and sterility in which women like Morag find themselves wedded to. In a pattern of almost exact repetition, her daughter Pique too has inherited a part of her parents' sense of loss. In Vancouver, where she grows and studies, she seldom sees her father who has become an itinerant singer and she misses her roots a great deal. Homeless and restless for a long time, it appears that she is neither able nor willing to adjust to society. This pattern of deprivation and dispossession is further reinforced by images of death, disease and sterility throughout the novel such as the evocative description of the aborted child and the dumping lot in the second part of the novel called 'The Nuisance Grounds.' Jules Tonnerre's death nay reported suicide due to the agony caused by throat cancer; and his sister Piquette's awful end by fire are both symbolic of the cruel victimization of the natives. But Laurence, while rejecting a romantic fusion of the red and white worlds in her handling of these relationships, does grant Morag a more comprehensive and meaningful understanding of herself and her world when towards the end of the novel, she takes a deliberative decision not to visit 'Sutherland where her people came from.' She tells Dan MacRaith, her old lover, that "It is a deep land here, all right. But it is not mine, except a long way back. I always thought it was the land of my ancestors, but it is not." As observed by a critic named Paul Hjartson, "with these words Morag locates her past, locates herself, in the world of Christie's stories where I was born. The myths are, in fact, now her reality: they structure her life; they are the means by which she designates herself and is designated as a subject." (*Crossing the Road*, p. 56)

Anita Desai's novel *Baumgartner's Bombay* too poses a similar problem as discussed above in Laurence's novel. In an interview with Andrew Robinson, Anita Desai has observed thus about the genesis of this novel: "All these years I have been searching for a way to return to my background, and only found the key a few years ago." The psyche of the protagonist Hugo Baumgartner is also shaped by his past and the narrative discourse becomes an attempt to escape the past for a meaningful present. But the real tragedy lies in his inability to come to terms with the situation so easily. The past incidents which are flashbacked become the backdrop of the present drama of Hugo's life that unfolds itself through the relationship with a female and former cabaret dancer named Lottee, Habibullah in Calcutta and Chaman Lal in Bombay. Baumgartner had come to India, as a young man to start a new life in business in this country. In reality, he was forced to leave Germany about fifty years ago when the atrocities on Jews in Nazi Germany (in the form of concentration camps) had become unbearable. We are told that one night there was violence in which Hugo's father was taken by force by some men and disappeared from Berlin. Returning after a fortnight, he died leaving behind him and his mother all alone. And ironically enough; Baumgartner's escape from the Nazi regime in Germany to India in search of a safe refuge leaves him bitter and completely disillusioned, as it was like a jump from one hell into another. If in Germany Hitler termed the Jews as 'Subhuman races in India, they were labelled as the 'hostile aliens.' Through a multi-focus spotlight on Hugo's life in the two metropolitan cities of Calcutta and Bombay, Desai unfolds the socio-cultural sterility of the two places. Here Calcutta has been very realistically depicted as the frivolous city of the bars, restaurants, race horses, cabaret dancers and 'the black-black streets' of the downtown, that becomes a simmering communal cauldron in the pre-partition days of India. Hugo's friend Habibullah comments rather stoically: "Every night they set some Muslim house on fire, stab some Muslim in the street, rob him too." The shadow-lines of communal riots as sketched in the novel appear to shift it to the contemporary scene where communalism, in one form or the other, stalks the streets of many Indian towns from time to time.

Hugo, however, meets his nemesis, in Bombay which according to Anita Desai 'is an abrasive city with its unrelieved ugliness, squall and noise. It is nothing but a poignant commentary on the degradation of human value-system, and the cruelty and callousness of the environment that an old man like Hugo caring for his pet cats is often made the butt of silly and funny jokes. In fact, by sketching the futility of Hugo's and Lotte's life in Bombay, Anita Desai's novel raises some pointed and patient questions regarding the status of an exile in a non-familiar milieu. Baumgartner's and Lotte's struggle for survival and the formidable focus operating around them certainly provide this novel a much deeper meaning. However, Hugo's life comes a full circle somewhat dramatically when he meets a young German named Kurt who looks to 'a certain type that Baumgartner had escaped and forgotten?' He tried to befriend this young man in order to overcome his loneliness though the latter was said to be generally hostile to everyone. This becomes the cause of his tragic death as he is murdered by the same youngman (German). After the death of Hugo, Lotte remains an isolated figure, totally broken after losing her oldest friend. The bunch of letters found by Lotte in Baumgartner's flat evocatively reveal the violence and cruelty of the concentration camps in the Nazi Germany. And this, with an extended meaning, becomes symptomatic of the cruelty and apathy of our times. In fact, Desai has herself pointed out in an interview: "There in just as much violence and cruelty going on in India. Baumgartner had left Germany and gone far away but never really left (escaped or could escape) crime and violence."

The contemporary socio-political situation in most parts of the world including India appears to point out clearly how prophetic a sensitive creative writer can be; and therein lies the true significance and achievement of Anita Desai's art as a novelist especially in *Baumgartner's Bombay.* Finally let me conclude by saying that Anita Desai and Margaret Laurence have both contributed significantly to the literary world by investing their works with a multicultural perspective that widens and enlarges the frontiers of thought and which is therefore considered a very important literary characteristic by most critics and thinkers as is evident from the following words of the Nobel-Laureate Derek Walcott: "To have loved one horizon is insularity; it blindfolds vision, it narrows experience."

The Theme of Disintegration: A Comparative Study of Anita Desai's *Cry, the Peacock* and Bharati Mukherjee's *Wife*

S. SUJATHA

There is today a considerable body of fiction in English written by Indians. In the last two decades, two women writers, Anita Desai and Bharati Mukherjee, have won world-wide recognition. There are other women writers like Kamala Markandaya, Ruth Prawer Jhabvala, Nayantara Sahgal and Shashi Deshpande who have made great strides but the kind of critical attention that has been given to Anita Desai and Bharati Mukherjee is unparalleled.

Anita Desai has to her credit nine novels, besides two collections of short stories. She won the prestigious Sahitya Akademi Award in 1978 for her novel, *Fire on the Mountain*, besides the Winifred Holby Award, and the Guardian Award. Her books have been short-listed for the Booker Prize. *In Custody* is now slated to be picturised by the famous Merchant Ivory combine which has brought Jhabvala's novels to the screen. Bharati Mukherjee's creative output consists of three novels *Wife, The Tiger's Daughter, Jasmine,* two works of non-fiction and two collections of short stories. It is with her winning the prestigious National Book Critics Award in 1988 for *The Middleman and Other Stories* that she has come into limelight.

In *Cry, the Peacock* and *Wife* there is a marked similarity with regard to the central episode they present. Maya in Anita Desai's novel and Dimple in Bharati Mukherjee's novel take the extreme step of killing their husbands. This final act is the culmination point of gradual disintegration of personality. While there are obvious points of similarity, there are also significant differences. What are the paths that the protagonists traverse before they reach the moment of catastrophe? Is there a tragic inevitability about the conclusion that both novelists reach?

The anguish in Maya's life may be traced to the fact that she believes surrender of self to be substraction from her personal freedom and wholeness. While Maya longs for love, she is at the same time afraid of involvement. Maya's unhappiness can be traced in part to external circumstances – her over-protected childhood and adolescence which makes it difficult for her to face the realities of adult life, the Oedipus complex for excessive love and dependence on her father which makes her seek a father substitute in her husband Gautama which obviously is not possible. This complex prevents her from achieving a satisfactory sexual relationship with her husband. Then there is her superstitious belief in the albino astrologer's prophesy – which predicted death after four years of marital life. More than the prophesy itself, her father's handling of the episode, the dismissal of ayah, the hounding out of the astrologer – make Maya push the disagreeable prophesy deep into her subconscious. The death of her pet dog Toto triggers her memory and once again she is caught up in the horror of the possibility of her imminent death. All these are the carefully woven mosaic of forces that undermine Maya's sense of well-being. But strictly speaking Maya's unhappiness is the product of her own consciousness. She is one of those highly sensitive creatures who are precariously balanced between reason and unreason. There is a tension in her, produced by her vibrant love of life and beauty and her obsessive fear of death.

Anita Desai's fictional prose is densely textured, enabling her to convey vividly Maya's sensuous delight in her surroundings. Her delight in textures, scents, sounds and even silence is palpable. It is this very love of life that increases her horror of 'non-being.' Anita Desai depicts the life of her protagonist Maya on two levels, the external and internal. At the external level, life is meaningless – because Maya's pervasive need for love, understanding, communion of souls she longs for, are not available. Gautama and Maya are not kindred souls. The kind of love that Cathreen and Heathcliff feel for each other, which makes it possible for Cathreen to declare so confidently "I am Heathcliff" is something Gautama cannot imagine even. There is gradual disenchantment, frustration, a sense of aloneness – which is almost existential in its intensity. Maya's neurosis deepens till the dividing line between sanity and insanity disappears. One of the most poignant features of the exploration of Maya's inner landscape is that Maya herself is conscious of her descent into madness. She is helpless to arrest it.

It is difficult to say at which precise point Maya decides that the death prophesied by the astrologer need not be hers but Gautama's. Thoughts of suicide turn into homicidal impulse. Gautama's fate is sealed.

In Mukherjee's novel, *Wife*, the problem between Dimple and her husband Amit Basu is one of communication, and an inability to come to terms with reality. Maya is a born rebel who cannot conform to society's dictates even in such a matter as the dress code, who finds no one in tune with her sensitive personality and tastes. Dimple is a far simpler character whose dreams are purely materialistic. All she wants out of life is a marriage to a neurosurgeon (a strange choice) and the luxuries of consumer society. She marries Amit, an engineer, who wants to immigrate to USA the golden land of opportunity. Her drab surroundings in Calcutta fill her with frustration but there is a difference in the quality of existential anguish experienced by Maya and the more pedestrian sense of frustration felt by Dimple.

Amit Basu successfully migrates to America but Dimple finds that it takes time to make good. Life is an uphill struggle where you are. Dimple is not a strong enough person to withstand the struggle. She does not have the required mental resilience. In fact her very name Dimple which the Oxford English Dictionary defines as 'a slight surface depression,' symbolizes her essential shallowness. To dismiss Dimple's predicament as solely due to failure to adjust with an alien culture, is too simplistic.

Dimple is a psychically disturbed person—even as Maya is though the causes are different. Depression is a serious mental ailment which has been depicted with great skill by both the novelists. The stages of disenchantment with their situation in life, frustration, the onset of neurosis, the gradual but perceptible building up of mental tension till the final link with sanity is snapped—this is common to both the novels.

The interesting deviation is why does Dimple kill her husband and Maya kill Gautama? Have the novelists in question laid enough foundation in the early parts of their novels to make the tragic conclusion inevitable?

In *Cry, the Peacock*—a novel which uses imagery as a mode of expression—the very title hints at the tragic end—for the peacocks which cry 'pia, pia' end by destroying themselves and their loves. In *Wife* there are enough ominous signs. The visions of abortion, killing of the foetus, a violent act against herself and her husband, the savagery with which Dimple kills a mouse, one notices that violence is out of all proportion to the object being killed:

> "I'll get you" she screamed. "There's no way out of this my friend." She seemed confident now, a woman transformed. And in an outburst of hatred, her body shuddering, her wrist taut with fury, she smashed the top of a small gray head.[1]

Both the women go through mental trauma which allows them no peace. The sense of violence and aggression is heightened in *Wife* by the pervasive violence of American life. Dimple confesses that in America talking about murders was like talking about weather. Anita Desai similarly refers to the pervasive spirit of violence in the cities.

While Maya is resigned to her arid marital life, Dimple makes a pitiful attempt to prove to herself that she is attractive to men by an affair with Milt Glasser. She realizes soon enough that it merely makes her more miserable.

The actual act of murder is achieved in startlingly different ways in the two novels under study. Maya plans and carries out Gautama's murder in a chillingly casual way. With a kind of composure, clarity of mind and purpose that the mad sometimes display, Maya lures Gautama to the terrace and in a sudden burst of fury, because Gautama stood between her and moon-light, she pushes him off the terrace to his death. She tries to rationalize the act, justifying it to herself by saying that Gautama is so uninvolved with life that he does not savour it—he merely exists—so death will not make a real difference. Maya's descent into total madness, her regression into childhood, and eventual death are accomplished with tremendous compactness.

Dimple's murder of her husband is presented in soft focus. It seems to take place in a neurotically charged atmosphere which is almost surrealistic:

> She sneaked up on him and chose a spot, her favorite spot just under the hairline, where the mole was getting larger and browner, and she drew an imaginary line of kisses because she did not want him to think she was the impulsive, foolish sort who acted like a maniac just because the husband was suffering from insomnia. She touched the mole very lightly and let her

> fingers draw a circle around the delectable spot, then she brought her right hand up and with the knife stabbed the magical circle once, twice, seven times, each time a little harder. (212-13)

One wonders if Dimple's stab seven times is some kind of weird reenactment of the marriage ritual where the couple take seven steps together. She seems to be symbolically destroying the marriage bond.

Anita Desai in *Cry, the Peacock* and Bharati Mukherjee in *Wife* thus present the theme of disintegration, with variation no doubt. The theme in both the novels has implications beyond the tragedy of the protagonists. Bharati Mukherjee's treatment suggests that Dimple's predicament transcends that of an individual enmeshed in the limbo of cultural shock, Anita Desai's protagonist faces the predicament of the tragic isolation of the individual and consequent sense of the absurdity of human life.

NOTE

1. Bharati Mukherjee, *Wife* (Penguin Books, 1990), p. 35.

Yasmine Gooneratne's *A Change of Skies* and Bharati Mukherjee's *Jasmine*: The Immigrant Experience in Australia and the USA

INDIRA NITYANANDAM

"He who crosses the ocean may change the skies above him, but not the colour of his soul," (167) writes Edward in his diary in 1887 at Badagini in Australia. Strangely enough, the place got its name from the Sinhalese word 'Badagini' which means 'hunger' or more literally 'fire in the belly.' Emigrants, now called expatriates, are obviously not rare or new in Australia. *A Change of Skies* by Yasmine Gooneratne traces the experiences of the linguistics expert Bharat Davasinha and his wife Navaranjini after Bharat accepts a visiting professorship at Southern Cross University in New South Wales. Running parallel to their experience are those of Bharat's grandfather Edward who reached the Australian shores on the S.S. Devonshire in 1882. Fleeing from a strict father, the rich and respected Mudaliyar of Walauwa and an unsuccessful love affair with his cousin Emily, Edward travels incognito – in fact, as the younger brother of the servant boy Devith. In the cramped conditions of the ship, he works to pay for his passage. In editing the diary maintained by Edward throughout the journey to and stay in Australia, Bharat and his wife discover the common threads that underline all expatriate experience. The novel presents the experience from three points of view – Edward's, Bharat's and Navaranjini's.

Jyoti Vidh – Jasmine – Jase – Jane and even Kali are the various names adopted by the protagonist of Bharati Mukherjee's third novel *Jasmine*. A simple peasant girl from Hasnapur in rural Punjab, Jyoti becomes Jasmine when she marries Prakash, a modern city man who believes in trashing traditions and declares impatiently: "There's no room in modern India for feudalism." (76) Jyoti thinks of Prakash as Prof. Higgins who can break "the Jyoti I'd been in Hasnapur and make a new kind of city woman. To break off the past, he gave me a new name; Jasmine . . . Jyoti, Jasmine: I shuttled between identities." (177) An identity change which begins thus continues for Jasmine when stunned by the sudden and brutal killing of her husband by terrorists, she decides to fulfill his dream and visit the U.S. Bred in traditional, rural India, her mission now is to reach a university campus in Florida, lie down on his new, unworn suit and commit Sati. As Half Face says, "getting your ass kicked halfway around the world just to burn a suit. I never heard such a fool notion." (114) One can explain her decision only by having a glimpse into the type of society in which she grew up. As a girl-child she was almost strangled to death so that her parents can avoid later problems of marriage and dowry. Later, she finds the secluded life of widows intolerable. She sees her friend commit Sati rather than choose to live as a widow in rural Punjab. In that context, it is hardly surprising that she is willing to travel to the U.S. at any cost—on a forged passport, with underworld travelling companions, raped by a scarred stranger in an unknown motel etc. Taking on the dreaded form of Kali, biting her tongue to allow blood ooze out, she kills him in demonaic fashion. She then sets out to face the world and the country of her dreams. Travelling the length and breadth of the U.S.—Professorji, Lillian Gordon, Wylie and Taylor and then Bud and Du are her family at different stages. As Jasmine says, "I have had a husband for each of the women I've been, Prakash for Jasmine, Taylor for Jase, Bud for Jane, Half Face for Kali." (197)

The expatriate writers face a multi-cultural situation which may be combined with a personal anguish due to discrimination or a sense of rootlessness, if rejected by their host countries. As coloured expatriates, both Bharati Mukherjee and Yasmine Gooneratne are likely to have faced their full share of racial discrimination. In spite of being married to a Canadian, Mukherjee's experiences in Canada were far from pleasant. In fact, she took the risk of quitting her job and shifting to the U.S. Yasmine Gooneratne has been living in Australia for the last twenty years and her personal experiences as an immigrant have coloured the protagonist. She is able to project the cultural confusion and confrontation of a multi-racial society. The clash of culture and the need for adaptation is a part of all expatriate experience.

Both these novels approach the expatriate experience in different ways: Gooneratne deals with the theme more seriously than does Mukherjee. Early in the novel, she describes the misconceptions that one has of the host country; the meagre knowledge of Australia based on a poster in a Geography class, the land of Kangaroos, on the frontiers of the civilized world. In fact, they view their stay there as a temporary exile, from where they will return at the end of five years. As Bharat's sister Vera warns them: "You'll be miserable. There's nothing there but Koalas and Kangaroos. And, the white Australia Policy?" To most Sri Lankans, the U.S. could be the land of their dreams but never Australia. It is the political and social unrest in their homeland that leads them to decide to move out. Strangely, a bad traffic jam on a busy morning is the last straw for Bharat and he accepts the offer from the University of New South Wales. To Jasmine, the U.S. is her dreamworld and her strange mission is soon forgotten. She sheds her Indian name and dress and adapts herself easily to every circumstance of life. In spite of occasional memories of life in India, she is never tormented by the clash of traditional Indian values and the American world she faces. Chameleon-like, she transforms herself. She exemplifies Mukherjee's 'Maximalist' creed which is essential, according to her, for every expatriate. According to her, they are neither nostalgic for their personal past nor afraid of their unfamiliar present. Bharat and his wife are different because thoughts of the home and land left behind are ever present in their lives. The political and social scenario of the homeland is hinted at in *A Change of Skies*. In *Jasmine* the increasing terrorism plays an important role as that is responsible for Jasmine's husband Prakash's sudden death.

Some Australians take kindly to the Asians and regard them "as exotics who are having difficulty sending roots into alien ground" (87) like the bluebells from England or the immigrant Mynah and Crow. The friendly Maureen warns Navaranjini, "I think it'll take exactly five years for the two of you to feel at home in Australia." (85) The locals expect the expatriates to change and harbour strange notions about the immigrants. The uneven height of their 4 poster bed is considered responsible for their healthy marital relationship. The Annual University Day turns out to be a money spinner due to Navaranjini's book exhibition and the prize attraction is naturally the *Kamasutra*. Bharat is seen as a human encyclopaedia containing information on everything Asian from "Abu Ben Adhem to Zen."

(215) In seeking ways to be assimilated, a change of name seems to be the first step. Australians quickly trim or truncate all proper nouns and hence Mangala Davasinha (Bharat) became Mangala Day and then Mundy, thus retaining neither the sound or the sense of the original name. Bharat naturally becomes Barry. The musical-sounding Navaranjini is chopped to Jean.

At the other end of the scale, we have another Sri Lankan who approaches the immigrant experience with great seriousness and doesn't see the funny side at all. He loves to be known by his full name; the pompous sounding Mekaboru Kiyanahati Balapan Koyako. He is considered a leader of the Sri Lankan community in Australia. In *Jasmine* we have a similar character – Prakash's ideal guru Prof. Devinder Vadhera which now sounds like David O. Hara. Rather than accept failure and return to India, the esteemed Professor was actually a sorter and importer of human hair. Like the Koyakos, he and his family hold on to everything Indian. "They let nothing go lest everything be lost." This made it impossible for them to be assimilated into the new culture. Little wonder then that Jasmine quits the place as she begins to feel claustrophobic.

The expatriate faces the dilemma of being unable to return home and yet not finding a home in the adopted land. He nurtures the hope that he will be able to merge into the culture of the new land. They change names, clothes and even partners in the case of Jasmine. She runs off with one man when she is pregnant with another man's child. No wonder Jasmine says, "I had been reborn" (163) – a total change from the girls of Punjab. This concept of rebirth in one life is repeatedly used by Mukherjee in this novel. Borrowing from Sant Kabir's well-known couplet of water mingling with water, she uses the metaphor of air to indicate merging with the total experience of the new country. "I took in everything," (179) admits Jasmine. A large dose of Hindu philosophy figures in this concept of the self mingling with the Absolute. Mukherjee firmly believes that the multi-cultural U.S. welcomes all immigrants, irrespective of colour and race. Hence, after the initial, brutal assault, Jasmine faces no discrimination of any sort. Taylor and Bud Ripplemeyer lean on her and Jasmine too takes their every wish as a command. She is confident: "I had landed and was getting rooted." (179)

The expatriate faces another difficult situation when he decides to visit home. "We would not behave like expatriates," (259) decide Jean and Barry before they go home on a visit. "Expats make scenes, expats complain about the food being 'off' in expensive hotels. Expats make fools of themselves by losing their tempers," (262) is the usual opinion. Even the mundane and the accepted begin to seem strange on a visit home. A number of reasons including the mindless ethnic violence in Sri Lanka strengthen their resolve to go back to Australia. In a serious vein, *A Change of Skies* describes the condition of creative artists of exiles for whom "exile can often result in a kind of death" (284) believe some. To Gooneratne, this expatriate experience can actually give us "an awareness that everything around us is caught up in a process of profound and inexorable change and that we are not only changing with it but are being perpetually remade." (285) As Edward has written on the tombstone of his friend: "Subject to change are all component things." (285)

How much time does it take for an unfamiliar landscape to invade an individual's mind, take possession of his imagination and change the colour not only of his words but of his soul? (280). In every expatriate's experience "there must surely have been a moment, a small space in time . . . when the anchor was let down, the sails folded, the landing made." (151) 'Acculturation' or adoption of changes in external behaviour begins early enough but 'assimilation' or the ability to react instinctively and emotionally to a culture is a far slower process. Breaking away from one's ethnicity and absorbing the new culture is the only way for survival, suggest both the novels. A genetic transformation makes it possible for Jane to decide "to reposition the stars." (240) For Jean and Barry's daughter "is allowed to grow up in a new country, free of the burdens of the past." (321) "The experience of exile opens beyond the limits of education." (285)

NOTES

1. Yasmine Gooneratne, *A Change of Skies* (New Delhi: Penguin, 1991).
2. Bharati Mukherjee, *Jasmine* (New Delhi: Viking, 1989).

Cross-Cultural Crisis in Bharati Mukherjee's *Jasmine* and *The Tiger's Daughter*

SHOBHA SHINDE

Cultural alienation is a world phenomenon today. The tremendous difference between two ways of life, leads a person to a feeling of depression and frustration. This could be called culture shock. When a person leaves his own culture and enters another, his old values come into conflict with the new ones he finds. Bharati Mukherjee has claimed: "We immigrants have fascinating tales to relate. . . . My aim is to expose Americans to the energetic voices of new settlers in this country." She describes the American experience as one of "fusion" and immigration a "two-way process" in which both the whites and the immigrants grow by the interchange and experience.

In her novels *Jasmine*[1] and *The Tiger's Daughter,*[2] Bharati Mukherjee has shown a dual cultural shock. Jasmine and Tara leave their respective countries in search of their dreams. This migration or "cultural transplant" leads to a crisis of identity and a final reconciliation to the choice. Bharati Mukherjee has deliberately avoided the immigrant writer's temptation to fall in the trap of glorifying his native country and to belittle and degrade the adopted country. She has presented a fascinating study of the problem of a displaced person in America as well as India. Jasmine leaves India in search of the American Dream while Tara nostalgically plans a trip to India in search of the Indian dream. The object of this paper is to present these two objective stances taken by Bharati Mukherjee and final disillusionment in store for her protagonists.

Jasmine's fate had been predicted by an astrologer very early in her life. He had foretold widowhood and exile with the forewarning that nobody could escape from his or her fate. Her journey through life led Jasmine through many transformations – Jyoti, Jasmine, Jase and Jane through large geographical locales like Punjab, Florida,

New York, Iowa and finally towards California. At every stage of her life Jasmine revolted against her fate and the path drawn for her.

The narrative shifts between the past and present, between India of her earlier life and America of the present. The past is Jyoti's childhood in the small village of Hasanpur, Punjab, her marriage to Prakash, the young ambitious city man, who always thrashed traditions. Pygmalion-like he had given her a new identity and new name Jasmine for she was small, sweet and heady and would quicken the whole world with her perfume.

The present was her life as Jane in Iowa, where she was a live-in-companion to Bud Ripplemeyer, a small-town banker. Bud was fascinated by her foreignness, but he never asked her about India. It scared him. He courted her because she was alien. She was darkness, mystery, inscrutability. "The past plugs me into instant vitality and wisdom. I rejuvenate him simply by being who I am." (200)

The American experience shocked Jane and disgusted her many a time:

> This country has so many ways of humiliating, of disappointing. . . . There are no harmless, compassionate ways to remake oneself. We murder who we were so we can rebirth ourselves in the images of dreams.

In the process of her transformation, Jane was seized by a longing to belong. She closely identifies herself with Bud's adopted son "Du" a Vietnamese because he was an immigrant like herself. Both had seen death closely. "They had both hurtled through time tunnels, seen the worst, and survived. Like creatures in fairy tales we've shrunk, we've swollen and we've swallowed the cosmos whole." (240)

Both Du and Jasmine were in a hurry to become American. They tried to forget the nightmares of their early lives. Assimilation in America was easy. They had just to start letting go. "Let go just one thing like not wearing our normal clothes, or a turban or not wearing the tikka on the forehead – the rest goes on its own down a sinkhole."

America, the land of dreams had many disillusions in store for her. Lillian Gordon, a kind Quaker lady in Florida, offered her a home, and also to several illegal immigrants. "The world's misery was a challenge to her ingenuity." This good Samaritan was tried in the American Court for harbouring undocumenteds. In New York, Jasmine was shocked by the sight of beggars, one of whom cursed her as a "foreign bitch" when she refused him alms. The taxi driver in New York was a migrant doctor from Kabul, who lived like dogs, because they had taken everything from them. On the streets of New York Jasmine saw more greed and more people like herself, "New York was an archipelago of ghettos seething with aliens." (140)

The experience with the Professor's family was even more frustrating: "I was spiralling into depression being the fortress of Punjabiness in their house. . . . In Flushing I felt immured. An imaginary brick wall popped with barbed wire cut me off from the past and kept me from breaking into the furture. I was a prisoner doing unreal time."

The biggest shock to Jasmine was the truth of the Professorji's means of earning a livelihood. He was not a Professor but an importer and sorter of human hair. America had not robbed him of his self-respect. "He needed to work here, but he didn't have to like it. He had sealed his heart when he'd left home. . . . He was a ghost hanging on." (153)

The next identity of Jase was thrust on her by the Hayse's family, where she worked as a "care-giver." The twist given to the narrative where Jase falls in love with Taylor is a weak link in the chain of events. The transformation of Jyoti had come half-circle: "Jyoti was now a sati-goddess. Jasmine lived for the future, for Vijh and wife and Jase lived for today. For every Jasmine the reliable caregiver there is a Jase, the prowling adventurer." (176)

Bharati Mukherjee supplements Jasmine's immigrant experiences with similar experience of Letita from Trinidad, and Jamaica from Barbados. Letita grumbled: "Slavery making a big comeback?" (179) While Jamaica cried her heart out every night because she was too proud to return back to her native country, Jane was shocked by the switching of relationships in America.

> In America nothing really lasts. I can say that now, and it doesn't shock me. But I think it was the hardest lesson of all for me to learn. We arrive so eager, to learn, to adjust, to participate, only to find the monuments are plastic, agreements are annulled. Nothing is forever, nothing is so terrible or so wonderful, that it won't disintegrate. (81)

The final crisis of the book comes when Jane is confronted with the souring of the American dream, through the suicide of Darrel. Du's departure from home in search for his family, destabilizes her. She is caught between her duty towards the cripple Bud and her love for Taylor. She makes the final choice. She doesn't feel guilty, but relieved. She has stopped thinking of herself as Jane. She feels potent enough once again to reposition her stars. Time would draw its own conclusions about her true identity. "Adventure, risk transformation—the frontier is pushing indoors. She cries through all the lives she has lived and for all her dead. . . . I am out of the door . . . greedy with wants and reckless with hope."

II

As in *Jasmine, The Tiger's Daughter* also reflects the confrontation between illusion and reality. But *The Tiger's Daughter* had adopted the technique of documentation to bring out the contrast between two worlds and two attitudes. An immigrant away from home idealizes his home country and cherishes nostalgic memories of it. Tara, was packed off by her father at early age of fifteen for America, because he was prompted by suspicion and pain about his country. Tara is homesick in Poughkeepsie. Little things pained her. She sensed discrimination if her roommate did not share her mango chutney. She defended her family and her country vehemently. She prayed to Kali for strength, so that she would not break down, before the Americans. New York was extraordinary and it had driven her to despair: "On days when she had thought she could not possibly survive, she had shaken out all her silk scarves, ironed them and hung them to make the apartment more Indian." (34)

It was fate that she fell in love with an American. Both the novels begin with a reference to fate and astrology. It seems a device adopted by the writer around which she can weave her plots. Tara's husband David was painfully Western, she was dutifully devious in her marriage. She could not communicate the finer nuances of her family background and life in Calcutta. Her husband asked naive questions about Indian customs and traditions. She felt completely insecure in an alien atmosphere. "Madison Square was unbearable and her husband was after all a foreigner."

After a gap of seven years Tara planned a trip to India, for years she had dreamed of this return. She believed that all hesitations, all shadowy fears of the time abroad would be erased quite magically if she could return home to Calçutta. With the precision of a newspaper reporter, Bharati Mukherjee leads her heroine through a series of adventures and misadventures to a final self-realization and reconciliation. Tara's homesick eyes noticed many changes in the city of Calcutta. She was outraged, and could not respond to these changes. She longed for the Bengal of Satyajit Ray, children running through cool green spaces, aristocrats despairing in music rooms of empty palaces. What confronted her was a restive city which forced weak men to fanatical defiance or dishonesty. Calcutta was losing its memories in a bonfire of effigies, buses and trams. An appetite for the grotesque had taken over the city: "Tragedy was not uncommon in Calcutta. The newspapers were full of epidemics, collusions, fatal quarrels and starvation, stretching before her was the vision of modern India." (117)

The writer interlinks the events – like Tara's visit to a funeral pyre at the river bank, her meeting a small beggar girl afflicted with leprosy, the vision of beggar children eating off the street, the superficialities in the lives of her friends, the riots and demonstrations and her claustrophobic rape by the politician Tuntunwala – to bring out the trauma of Tara's visit to India. Tara's visit to Darjeeling is also marred by ugly and violent incidents.

Many of Tara's doubts and conflicts are resolved by the strength, determination and quiet dignity of her parents. Antonia Whitehead an American lends Tara a fresher and clearer perspective about her own country. Antonia Whitehead had decided to make India her home, for she believed that India needed help. Tara realized that her earlier responses to Calcutta had also been similarly impatient, menacing and equally innocent. The visit to the ashram of Mata Kananbala Devi makes her share her love for her mother as well as the worshippers. The Indian dream is shattered but the writer leads the heroine to a final reconciliation: "Camac street had felt the first stirrings of death. With new dreams like Nayapur, Tara's Calcutta was disappearing. New dreams occurred with each new bull-dozer incision in the green romantic hills. Slow learners like Tara were only victims." (199)

At the end of the novel, Tara is involved in a violent demonstration, in which Joyob Roy Chawdhury, a symbol of the old world order is brutally beaten to death. Pronob the youth tries to save him, but is himself injured in the process. This was a course of history which could not be stopped. "She felt she had made peace with the city, nothing more was demanded." (202)

III

A close experience of both the worlds – the Western and the Indian – gives Bharati Mukherjee an authentic and objective perspective with a delicious combination of malice, charm, irony and sympathy. She pushes both her heroines to the edges of their worlds, and liberates them for a new world order. One can question whether being an immigrant has been a deterrent to Mukherjee's own creativity as she remains devoid of the stability afforded by one's roots. But it cannot be denied that hers is a voice which demands our attention and respect.

NOTES

1. Bharati Mukherjee, *Jasmine* (New Delhi: Penguin, 1990).
2. Bharati Mukherjee, *The Tiger's Daughter* (London: Chatto and Windus, 1973).

Sado-Masochism as a Literary Device in Bharati Mukherjee's *Wife*

M. RAJESHWAR

Bharati Mukherjee's novel *Wife* stands out as a unique fictional work by virtue of its insightful probing into its heroine's psyche and its indubitable technical excellence. Surfacially *Wife* is the simple story of Amit and his wife Dimple, newly married Bengali immigrants to the USA. Dimple's ill-concealed sado-masochistic compulsions are soon precipitated by the violence-ridden and individualistic American life and culminate in her killing of her husband. This psychic development in Dimple has been variously but uncritically viewed as her desperate effort to 'forget' her Indian roots necessitated by the demands of American life and as her assertion of independence from her overbearing husband. In this paper I am going to argue that Dimple suffers from the neurotic compulsion of indulging in sado-masochistic acts in order to conceal her own sense of intrinsic weakness and failure.

Psychoanalytically speaking this defence strategy is known to be ubiquitously employed by masochists everywhere. And if they also have an added disadvantage of a clear predisposition to neurosis like Dimple, the problem is further confounded. The masochist-neurotic seems to convert even chance occurrences into painful experiences. He seems to ever deeply submerge himself in misery. The aim of all such masochistic suffering is satisfaction although it is hardly ever attained except in sexual fantasies and perversions of masochistic nature. Other forms of masochistic suffering serve only the purpose of narcotising the lesser forms of pain which we all encounter every day and deal with rationally.

Dimple appears to indulge in masochistic suffering in order to lull the pain of disappointment with life, especially with married life. She happened to set a high store on marriage: "Marriage, she was sure, would free her, fill her with passion. Discreet and virgin, she waited for real life to begin."[1] She hoped that marriage would offer her a different kind of life – "an apartment in Chowringhee, her hair done by Chinese girls, trips to New Market for nylon saris." (3) She longed so intensely for it that the years of waiting made her "nervous, . . . prone to colds, coughs and headaches." (3) She constantly imagined her future husband to be the very embodiment of the virtues of the commercial society:

> She borrowed a forehead from an aspirin ad, the lips, eyes and chin from a body-builder and shoulders ad, the stomach and legs from a trousers ad and put the ideal man by herself in a restaurant on Park Street or by the side of a pool at a five-star hotel. He wore blue bathing trunks, there was no ugly black hair on his back and shoulder blades as he leaped feet first into the pool while she stood on the edge in a scarlet sari with a gold border, behind wraparound sunglasses, and trailed her toes in the water. (23)

We very often see her obsessively measuring her husband against her ideal man and her life against her dream and finding both of them wanting in many respects and despairing as a result. While on one hand she tries hard to adjust to Amit's wishes and be a dutiful wife, she is never quite unaware of the fact that he is not the man of her dreams.

> She wanted to dream of Amit but she knew she would not. Amit did not feed her fantasy life; he was merely the provider of small material comforts. In bitter moments she ranked husband, blender, color TV, Cassette tape recorder, stereo, in their order of convenience. (113)

Her knowledge of the possibility of greater happiness with a different man ruins her attainable happiness with Amit within the marital relationship.

Life with him, both in India and America, is naturally a big disappointment for her. In her moments of feverish introspection she thinks that life has been cruel to her:

> Life should have treated her better, should have added and

> subtracted in different proportions so that she was not left with a chimera. Amit was no more than that. He did not feed her reveries; he was unreal. She was furious, desperate; she felt sick. (156)

Marriage has not "provided all the glittery things she had imagined, had not brought her cocktails under canopied skies and three A.M. drives to dingy restaurants where they sold divine *kababs* rolled in *roti*." (101-2) The cumulative effect of all these experiences or rather the lack of them renders her "incapable of love" (131) and leaves her a neurotic.

It is interesting to note why Amit is what he is. Like anybody who has made pragmatism a way of life he is unsentimental, quick and decisive in gestures, cautious in approach and meticulous in planning for future. But for his carefully cultivated pragmatism he wouldn't marry the flat-chested, short and wheatish Dimple who can speak only broken English. Like any traditionally brought up Indian husband, he does not know how to pay a compliment to his wife. He would like her to stay at home and attend to the household chores rather than go out, work and earn. In a word, he appears to be almost a personification of *Ego* in the Freudian sense. He constantly strives to achieve its ideals. The culture he is born into requires of him to earn and provide for future whatever be the cost and he withdraws his love and other emotional attachments from his wife in pursuit of the cultural aims. Freud has interesting things to say about this:

> The work of civilization has become increasingly the business of men, it confronts them with ever more difficult tasks and compels them to carry out instinctual sublimations. . . . Since a man does not have unlimited quantities of psychical energy at his disposal, he has to accomplish his tasks by making an expedient distribution of his libido. What he employs for cultural aims he to a great extent withdraws from women and sexual life. His constant association with men, and his dependence on his relations with them, even estrange him from his duties as a husband and father. Thus the woman finds herself forced into the background by the claims of civilization and she adopts a hostile attitude towards it.[2]

He adds in the same breath that under the cultural conditions of today the woman is not properly prepared during her formative years for her role as wife. The high premium set on the maintenance of female chastity prevents her from the danger of impulses of love which do not lead to marriage. Subsequently when she is freely allowed to love and live with a man she finds herself utterly uncertain of her feelings. Most often the marital relationship ends up in disappointments. In people like Dimple the disappointment invariably leads to the development of sado-masochistic tendencies. Female masochism is thus largely a culturally-determined phenomenon and should be understood as such. Dimple's masochism is of special interest in the sense that in view of her proneness to neurosis it also forms part of what Karen Horney calls the "general principle of finding satisfaction by losing the self"[3] in ever greater misery and it is practised by dissolving the individuality with all the doubts, conflicts, pains, limitations and isolation attendant on it. In case a wish for the extinction of the individual self assumes pathological proportions, and when it is coupled with sadism lurking in the unconscious as in the case of Dimple, it may either lead to the extinction of the physical self or the physical extermination of a perceived agent of pain. Therefore Dimple lives constantly under the shadow of death, sometimes having close brush with it. But mostly she lives out her masochistic drives in fantasies which saves her from complete self-obliteration and it also explains why she kills not herself but her husband at the end of the novel. But why only at the end? Here consideration of the technique becomes important.

Perhaps in order to lend further depth to the portrayal of Dimple, Bharati Mukherjee uses a rare fictional technique which was originally developed by Peter Brooks[4] on the basis of Freud's theories concerning instincts. In *Beyond the Pleasure Principle*, Freud defines an instinct as "an urge inherent in organic life to restore an earlier state of things,"[5] thus stressing their conservative nature. The operation of *thanatos* ensures that men return to elemental existence with a final extraordinary release of energy. *Eros* or the self-preservative group of instincts too contributes to this process by warding off the possible external ways of the organism's returning to lifelessness. In other words, they 'bind' the mobile energy of the libido to avert its premature discharge which usually leads to untimely termination of life. Based on these Freudian conceptualizations Peter Brooks postulates to the novels highly mobile textual energy which manifests in the form of high expectations raised at the beginning. Just as when the energy attached to *thanatos* is not properly tamed life itself ends before it hardly ever begins, a premature termination of expectancy – the danger of which lurks at every significant turn – will bring the text to an abrupt end while convention would see it through the normal course of exposition, conflict and resolution. It therefore happens that a middle or detour attends to building the mystery layer upon layer maintaining a forward swing of the story and bringing it to a finale where the final illumination comes about and is the most pleasurable.

Speaking in terms of the technique, *Wife* shows at several places all the portents of frittering off and losing narratable interest mainly in the form of threats to the life of the heroine. But the different fragments of the story are held together and treated to a logical conclusion by averting the death of Dimple. Just as an organism would return to inorganic state of existence after running a strenuous course of life "in its own fashion" and of reasons which are present in the organism itself, Dimple, being neurotic and thus readily submitting to analytic enquiry, returns symbolically to the state of lifelessness and the novel gradually builds up tension to the bursting point and discharges it in a torrent in the killing scene and ultimately ceases to be worthy of prolongation.

Freud has boldly declared that "the aim of all life [forms] is death."[6] Dimple's life is a long tryst with death. Her masochism makes her moribund consciousness look almost transparent. As her need to die increases in intensity, she becomes more and more neurotic and *vice versa*. However, death should also be viewed here as the logical and final goal of the conservative instincts in order to do justice for its employment as a literary device. It can therefore be understood that her awareness of death is partly a thematic necessity and partly an aesthetic necessity.

During her Calcutta days she has two important encounters with death – one symbolic, another actual. The first, her sadistic killing of a mouse, has a surrealistic touch to it. The incident occurs after Dimple has undergone a series of frustrating experiences which include especially her marriage to Amit. She ruthlessly chases the rodent and kills it with an uncalled-for show of anger.

> "I'll get you!" she screamed. "There's no way out of this, my friend." She seemed confident now, a woman transformed.

> And in an outburst of hatred, her body shuddering, her wrist taut with fury, she smashed the top of small gray head. (35)

And to her, the mouse looks pregnant which introduces the motif of pregnancy. Presumably Dimple herself is pregnant by this time. Such occasions to give a free play to her aggressiveness are few and far between—a point which calls for a little theoretical enquiry. Freud opines that part of the *thanatos* gets separated and is placed at the service of *Eros*, so that, the organism is destroying something else instead of itself. A restriction of aggression directed outwards proportionately increases self-destruction.[7] This is what seems to happen to Dimple. By the time she has her next brush with death, that of inflicting an abortion on herself, she outwardly passes from sadism to masochism. Although consciously she thinks of the pregnancy as a hurdle in her way to the USA, when properly understood, it becomes clear that it is a manifestation of masochism. Her masochism finds an eloquent expression through this slightly bizarre act. To add to this, her tendency to reject everything that falls outside the scope of her comprehension is perhaps responsible for her rejection of the pregnancy because, as she admits, nobody has consulted her "before depositing it in her body." (31) Symbolically speaking, in her rejection of the pregnancy she rejects Amit. A diminished inclination to have children is certainly a part of neurotic reaction. Technically speaking, the abortion marks a swing towards a premature suspension of the hopes raised at the beginning of the novel. The narrative has to be carried forward. Dimple survives the abortion but not before making her point. Procreation is the only way available to the organism to prolong life. In this act a tiny part of the organism gets separated and lives for a longer time and if uninterrupted by external agents the process goes on endlessly. Dimple registers her protest against this process by a premature termination of pregnancy. It also marks the first major symptom of her neurotic trouble. Things appear to be happening of their own accord—even the ones which are significant to her. Apart from effecting the abortion all that she could now do is to neurotically talk to herself, irritate and nag Amit for no apparent reason, suffer from insomnia, entertain occasional sadistic feelings and actually try sadism out on such harmless objects of beauty as a plastic flower. She thinks of her destruction of the Sens' flower as a "narrow escape" though she is not sure from what she has escaped or how. (105)

With the second part of the novel the scene moves to New York, the highest crime-prone city in the world. The New York life appears to prove particularly destructive to Dimple. First it sets her romantic notions about America at naught and then unusually activates her inwardly directed martido by constantly carrying to her gory murder stories. To Dimple, death appears to present itself in myriad forms. Sleepers look to her more like corpses than as people under temporary suspension of consciousness. Her friend Ina Mullick appears in her dream as dead which properly interpreted could mean that Dimple fervently wishes herself dead. It is a plain displacement contrived by dream-work:

> That night she had a new dream: she was walking on the beach. A crowd had gathered just ahead. Something strange had been washed upon the beach. A whale, a porpoise, a shark, she heard people say. She fought her way through a crowd that suddenly disappeared. At her feet lay Ina Mullick, *in Dimple's sari*, a thin line of water spilling from her mouth. (103, emphasis added)

The effect of constant proximity of death begins to severely tell upon her psyche. She finds herself collapsing inwardly, becomes terribly apprehensive of imaginary dangers, entertains premonitions and begins to gradually lose touch with reality. She just cannot understand what is happening to her for whatever is happening to her is doing so at the unconscious level and is therefore beyond her reach. When she sits down to list the reasons for her miserable predicament her mind goes blank:

> After he [Amit] had left the room she gave herself what she thought was probably half an hour, then switched on the table lamp, took a piece of paper and a ballpoint pen out of a drawer in the night table and listed the reasons why she was unhappy.
>
> 1. The plants were dying
> 2.
> 3.
> 4.
> 5.
>
> It was no use. . . . (179-80)

Since she is not sure of the source cf her trouble she turns with full force to self-destruction and devises at least ten different ways of ending her life under the central metaphor of her life as a "dying bonfire": getting her head caught in the oven, slicing open her jugular vein, consuming pesticide, getting suffocated in a garbage bag, starving, falling on bread-knife, getting her head hit with shovels and finally getting mugged and killed in the laundry room in the basement after midnight. Dimple, however, does not try out any of these methods although they are quite expressive of her gradually depleting psychic energy reserves. Her psychic apparatus puts up a self-preservative shield against her return to the inorganic state which also incidentally defers illumination of the novel in the technical sense.

To begin with, she uses such defence devices as verbal retorts against Amit, groundlessly blaming him of wanting her to die, temporarily withdrawing from the world (which is symbolically presented in the novel in the scene in which she retreats to a bench in the playground in front of the apartment building and stays there for many hours, (177) and occasionally day-dreaming of killing Amit. Her problems are however too stupendous to be tackled by ordinary defence machanisms. The next stage of defence process begins without her ever knowing it. She often finds herself doing things without her conscious will. One such incident is quite enlightening. It happens after Leni has offended her:

> After Leni removed her cup Dimple kept on pouring, over the rim of Leni's cup, over the tray and the floating dentures till the pregnant-bellied tea pot was emptied and Leni and Ina were standing and shaking her, "Dimple, Dimple, stop it!" (152)

Dimple can afford to be immediate and physical in her reaction with others like the above. With Amit she cannot be so dramatic. She has to repress a good deal of anger which keeps simmering in her unconscious all the time.

At a further remove, she begins to experience a split personality, sees her body and soul apart, manifests extreme self-consciousness and acutely suffers from imaginary illnesses: "But it was the imaginary ills that were impossible to treat. She felt moody and light-headed." (205) That marks the onset of psychosis.

During her psychotic spell the hitherto unthought of defence strategies are pressed into service while her death-bound journey takes her closer and closer to the end-point. Now that the *Ego's* hold on her is considerably relaxed, a clear pathological picture emerges. In this light, her seduction of Milt, her landlady's brother, in her own bedroom, can be interpreted as a desperate attempt by her diseased psyche to preserve her and stop her further deterioration. Freud has held that when there is a pathological masochistic configuration in a person the ethical considerations concerning sex are drowned so that the person indulging in these 'sinful' acts can be subsequently chastised by the conscience. And Dimple is hungry for that kind of punishment.

Secondly and most importantly, Dimple now begins to experience death at close quarters. She leaves all pretensions and begins to view herself as already dead, first in dream:

> An after-dream persisted when she woke up: someone had murdered her the night before and concealed her corpse among the Bedouin brasses and baskets of indoor plants. She wrapped her blue bathrobe tighter around her breasts and hips and did all the things she normally did between seven and eight on weekday mornings, but she knew that she was dead and that Amit would recoil from her as soon as he sat down at the table for his Wheaties and two fried eggs. (185-86)

And thereafter in wakefulness too she sees herself as dead and even the post-mortem performed on her body. She even wonders what Amit would do if she dies in New York. Will he cope with it as well as he could, back in Calcutta?

Her sado-masochist drives further compel her to inflict the same kind of punishment upon Amit which she wishes him to do her. In other words she wishes to die but by forming a reaction she kills Amit. Her killing of Amit with a kitchen-knife is the most longed-for, albeit unconsciously masochistic, event in her life. The incident occurs in a free-floating dream-like state and is rendered by the author in a virtually delirious style:

> She sneaked up on him and chose a spot, her favorite spot just under the hairline, where the mole was getting larger and browner, and she drew an imaginary line of kisses. . . . She touched the mole very lightly and let her fingers draw a circle

> around the delectable spot, then she brought her right hand up and with the knife stabbed the magical circle once, twice, seven times, each time a little harder, until the milk in the bowl of cereal was a pretty pink and the flakes were mushy and would have embarrassed any advertiser, and then she saw the head fall off—but of course it was her imagination because she was not sure anymore what she had seen on TV and what she had seen in the private screen of three A.M. and it stayed upright on the counter top, still with its eyes averted from her face, and she said very loudly to the knife that was redder now than it had ever been when she had chopped chicken and mutton with it in the same kitchen and on the same counter, "I wonder if Leni can make a base for it; she's supposed to be very clever with her fingers."
>
> Women on television got away with murder. (212-13)

Having thus killed Amit, Dimple has ultimately succeeded in achieving a modicum of satisfaction for masochistic drives. She has turned the whole society into a punishing agent. Society will never forgive her for killing a dutiful husband and there is also the law to contend with. It will treat Dimple as any ordinary criminal and may even award her the death sentence. And as though that is not enough, by a trick of fantasy she has in effect killed herself through this act. In this sense her masochistic drives are fully satisfied, a thing which rarely happens in psychoanalytical history.

She has all along been firmly set on her way to death whether viewed in terms of the artistic requirements of the novel or her rather peculiar mental frame. A close attention to the inner dynamics of the novel would dispel any doubts in arriving at this conclusion. The narrative, for example, is so full of morgue imagery that the reader is reminded of death on almost every page. That death has been delayed so long is a fact which comes as a big surprise to us. Dimple has been allowed to use all the devices available to an organism to preserve itself. It is only when further prolongation is not possible that death occurs in such concrete shape.

To put it in different words, the technique employed by the author, has brought the narrative to an impassable halt after holding the attention of the reader glued to it for the whole length of it. Just as Dimple has symbolically returned to the inorganic state of existence by the silent operation of *thanatos* the narrative too has come to a final dissolution as a result of its internal necessities. The ending in this sense does not appear to be contrived. It is quite in the logic of the narrative to come to this end with a final explosive release of the pent-up tension – an experience which is anticipated and pleasantly felt by every sensitive reader.

NOTES

1. Bharati Mukherjee, *Wife* (New Delhi: Sterling, 1976), p. 13.
2. Sigmund Freud, *Civilization and its Discontents*, trans. James Strachey (Harmondsworth: Penguin, 1964), p. 293.
3. Karen Horney, *The Neurotic Personality of Our Time* (New York: W.W. Norton, 1937), p. 270.
4. Peter Brooks, "Freud's Master Plot," *Literature and Psychoanalysis: The Question of Reading: Otherwise*, ed. Shoshama Felman (Baltimore: The Johns Hopkins Univ. Press, 1982), pp. 280-300.
5. Sigmund Freud, *Beyond the Pleasure Principle*, trans. James Strachey (London: Hogarth, 1974), p. 30.
6. *Ibid.*, p. 32.
7. Sigmund Freud, *Civilization and its Discontents*, p. 310.

"Splintered Self": An Approach to Bharati Mukherjee's *Wife*

S. INDIRA

Modernism in literature calls for a cumulative exploration of the inner dimension of characters as modern age stresses the restless, questing spirit of man. With an increasing dominance of "mimesis over diegesis,"[1] dramatizing the inner world of characters instead of narrating the events with objective realism, the modern novel becomes an interesting literary exercise. Replacing coherence and causality in narrative structure, a note of indeterminacy pervades the modern novel generating "plurality of meaning."[2] The authorial voice is suppressed and so is the autonomy of individual self. Instead, the modern note of disillusion, fragmentation and solipsism is persistently heard.

Bharati Mukherjee's *Wife* falls into the category of the modern novel as it presents an intense inner world of neurotic and solipsistic individual using symbols as 'centering nodes.' Instead of trying to combine the freedom of the individual with tolerance for fellow-beings, Bharati Mukherjee chooses to glorify the alienated individual. Rootlessness and unreal existence are the main concerns of this expatriate novelist who has set out to make a deliberate distortion of Indian womanhood. Her women characters are tantalized by the possibility of passion, which they mistake for love and self-expression, in America which appears to be a free land, a veritable dream-land for all Indian girls.

Dimple (the name sounds more Western than Indian), the protagonist in *Wife* is an extremely immature girl who constantly dreams of marriage as she hopes that it would bring freedom and love. At the same time she is not clear about the concepts of freedom and love. This ambiguity underlying her mental make-up defines the incompleteness of her very being. After an excruciatingly painful waiting which makes her desperate and suicidal, she is finally married to Amit Kumar Basu, an average middle-class, unimaginative, young engineer who dreams of making a fortune in America and retiring to live a comfortable rich life in Calcutta. But, soon after her marriage, she feels cheated as her romantic, adolescent mind cannot grasp the reality that freedom too has certain limitations. She begins to resent her new home, her in-laws and even her husband who doesn't seem to be capable of feeding her fantasy-life. At this stage, when she begins to reconstruct her 'ideal' man from faces from magazines, unable to identify herself with anyone in the family, the prospect of becoming a mother enrages her. She treats it as an outrage on her body and induces an abortion, disposing of that "tyrannical and vile" thing deposited in her body. She justifies herself by arguing that she cannot afford to take any relics from her old life to America where she hopes to begin life afresh and become a more exciting person. But, once again, even after going to America, her hopes are belied. She feels that the temporary joblessness has made Amit collapse inwardly and become frail losing his erstwhile infallible position in the family. She is further shaken by the knowledge that America with all its outward glitter allows Indian wives only to create 'little Indias' around them but does not allow them either freedom or fulfilment as evident in the case of Ina Mullick who, despite her attempts at becoming 'a total American,' remains a frustrated individual. After this disturbing realization, Dimple sinks into a world of isolation, unable to welcome the bright prospect of setting up a new home even after Amit gets a job. After a few pathetic attempts to merge herself into the new culture by wearing the borrowed outfit of Marsha and by flirting with Milt Glasser, Dimple experiences total estrangement from herself and her surroundings as well. Torn by the conflict between her fantasy world and the reality of her situation, she allows her mind to be totally conditioned by the commercials on T.V. and magazines so much so she loses the ability to distinguish them from the world of reality. Caught in a whirlwind of traumatic emotions, her tradition questioning her outrageous adultery, her present confused self wishing to become American by any means, Dimple finally kills Amit to suppress her guilty conscience and also to feel very American, almost like a character in a T.V. serial.

Bharati Mukherjee presents the world of Dimple, a world of day-dreams and nightmares and her morbid psyche through a series of grotesque images. Dimple's morbidity is evident while she is still at her parental home in the way she allows her conscious mind to be completely dominated by the colourful romance projected in the advertisements and stories of magazines. Indulging herself in sexual fantasies with cricket stars, young cabinet ministers and heroes from novels, Dimple sets out on a long journey of unreal, meaningless and morbid existence. As she has projected herself as a "sweet and docile" (14) girl in her parental home, even her parents are not aware of her schizophrenic nature. They just remain as flat characters, never intruding into the inner reverberations of their daughter's mind.

One cannot justify Dimple's morbid imagination and insane behaviour even on the basis of her immaturity. After many passionate assertions that she would like to experience all the pain and loyalty of Sita, she ought to have welcomed the prospect of motherhood. But, it looks as though she is a fragmented personality, while one part of her wants to emulate traditional images, the other self revels in morbid musings. The vision of neurosurgeons "dressed in spotless white, peering into opened skulls," (3) a day-dream fed on her romantic imagination coupled with a penchant for the grotesque has now turned into a sinister vision of abortionists, "men with broken teeth and dirty fingers who dug into her body." (33) She does not belong to the world of reality any more. What ought to have been real is not real to her. "Vomiting was real to her, but pregnancy was not." (31) The vision she conjures up for her unborn baby, "one with wrinkled skin like a very oldman's and large head filled with water," (41) is so cruel that one cannot help wondering about the novelist's capacity for creating such outrageous images. Dimple's obsessive fascination with her vomit, her pride and joy in the very act of vomiting are terribly revolting. Justifying to herself that the baby would hinder her chances of becoming 'a more exciting person' abroad, she skips her way to abortion thinking that it is not a murder after all. While "the dead baby lizard" (7) found in her pillow case in her parental home foregrounds this macabre act, the swollen mouse she kills with an unreasonable ferocity symbolizes her own pregnant self—"to Dimple, the dead mouse looked pregnant." (35) This incident also hints at the homicidal tendency of Dimple that makes the reader apprehensive.

Love and death are the most important things to Dimple as in the case of Maya of Anita Desai's *Cry, the Peacock*. While it is the dance of peacocks that defines the tragic predicament of Maya which chimes in with many other images of dance, it is America that allures Dimple into believing that it stands for love and death. Right from the very first day of her arrival in New York, all that Dimple hears from people and sees on the T.V. is about muggings, rape, murder – an aspect of the new world that seems to hold an inexplicable but unending fascination for immigrant-residents like Jyoti Sen. Being an incurable fantasizer and addict to the bright colourful world of advertisements, Dimple falls an easy victim to the various magazine and T.V. ads. She accepts them literally and one example, sufficient to speak volumes about her total lack of maturity and depth, is a magazine ad which exhorted people to "express" themselves in their "surroundings":

> Express yourself in your surroundings. Discover your own grand passion and indulge it to excess. Then simplify the rest, throw out, be ruthless. That's the secret to happiness. (87)

Fascinated and inspired by this ad, Dimple looks at Sen's apartment, which she found lovely before, with distaste as now it seems to her only 'convenient.' Perhaps, it is the other part of the ad she is trying to follow when she strikes an illicit relationship with Milt Glasser in a passionate attempt to find an identity in America. In wearing Marsha's clothes and shoes, in borrowing English words from Ina and Milt even to quarrel with her own husband, in devising various extravagant, mercenary schemes to commit suicide and to murder Amit, Dimple seems to be indulging in her passion to become a new woman and lead a very free, exciting life as the soap-operas on T.V. show. She even tries to justify herself after killing Amit: "Women on television got away with murder." (213)

Though she is at times shocked at her own intensity of feeling and her capacity to hate, eventually Dimple exorcises her ungratified passion through violence alone. Neither the cultural conflict nor a feminine need for freedom can account for Dimple's bizarre, blasphemous responses. As a critic points out, "Dimple's problem is her utter rootlessness."[3] As she cannot come to terms with either her own culture or America's culture, she finds herself at cross-roads, and visualizes her life as "a dying bonfire." (119)

The total apathetic existence of Dimple, spending all the day time sleeping like an invalid, and her fears and confusion at having no still point within her consciousness, fail to evoke pity or sympathy in the reader, though he comes to understand the continuous laceration Dimple's self is subjected to. It is because the novel abounds in repulsive, revolting images of disease, crime and death, inviting scathing comment from critics. "The woman who sees such things around and the mind which creates are one and the same with absolute disregard for the sanctity of art emotion."[4]

Though writers like Anita Desai and Shashi Deshpande also experimented with this "complexity" of inner experience, they are now engaged in creating a new self-hood, drawing sustenance from tradition and trying to arrive at a resolution of the dilemma within the family structure. One hopes that Bharati Mukherjee too moves in that positive direction. "The life and breath of the novel is found essentially in the tension and balance between the personal and the social,"[5] but not certainly in estrangement from society and dissociation from reality.

NOTES

1. David Lodge, *After Bakhtin* (London and New York: Routledge, 1990), pp. 25-44.
2. *Ibid.*, p. 86.
3. Jasbir Jain, "Foreignness of Spirit: The World of Bharati Mukherjee's Novels," *The Journal of Indian Writing in English*, vol. 13, no. 2, July 1985, pp. 12-19.
4. Rajini Ramachandra, "Bharati Mukherjee's *Wife*: An Assessment," *The Literary Criterion*, vol. 26, March 1991, p. 66.
5. Raymond Williams, "Realism and the Contemporary Novel," *Twentieth Century Literary Criticism*, ed. David Lodge (London: Longman, 1972), pp. 590-91.

From Acculturation to Self-Actualization: Diasporal Dream in Bharati Mukherjee's *Jasmine*

T. PADMA

Bharati Mukherjee, "the clear eyed but affectionate immigrant in American society,"[1] has become a celebrity for her distinctive approach to expatriatehood as a metaphysical experience of exile and as an agent of attitudinal change, both in the minority and majority cultures. Her concern transcends the run-of-the-mill-issues of culture shock and adjustment problems to encompass existential angst and zeitgeist.

Diasporal dream figures prominently in all her fiction, but its treatment after her settling in America seems to be more assured and more comprehensive in its coverage of the many moods of expatriation – nostalgia, frustration and hope than in the Canadian phase of her life where uncertainty and despondency prevailed, Bharati Mukherjee's glowing tribute to America as a country where "there is a kind of curiosity and exuberance" offers a glaring contrast to her pained outburst: "In Canada I was frequently taken for a . . . shoplifter, frequently assumed to be a domestic and praised by astonished auditors that I did not have a singsong accent."[2]

Bharati Mukherjee rightly sees an echo of this dejected state in the "pathetic and put upon"[3] appearance of the heroines of *Tiger's Daughter* and *Wife.* The shift to America wrought a sea-change in her personality and gave a new fillip to her literary aspiration. Her own acknowledgement of this is worth-noting: "For me it is a movement away from the aloofness of expatriation to the exuberance of immigration."[4]

Written in this frame of mind, *Jasmine* seems vibrant with Bharati Mukherjee's eager savouring of the bracing typical American reverence for the autonomy of the individual. Further, informed by

Bharati Mukherjee's special insight into American life – that of 'observer-participant' as Clark Blaise's wife – this novel has about it the authentic ring of an experience tested against the pulse of the author's existence. This does not mean that the novel is autobiographical. Bharati Mukherjee's own background in real life – top family, top school, top caste, top city – is worlds apart from that of her poverty-ridden heroine Jasmine, living in a shabby dwelling devoid of minimum amenities like water and electricity. The similarity therefore is, to use Bharati Mukherjee's words, in the "shape of her life" and of her "desires."[5] As one of the post-colonial writers, Bharati Mukherjee steers clear of Naipaul's love-hate relationship to his roots, Kureshi's impassioned decrying of racism and Cowasjee's defeatistic acceptance of a 'nowhereman' status. Her acknowledgement of her indebtedness to Malamud is worth-noting:

> I see a strong likeness between my writing and Bernard Malamud's in spite of the fact that he describes the lives of East European Jewish immigrants and I talk about newcomers from the Third World. Like Malamud I write about a minority community which escapes the ghetto and adapts itself to the patterns of the dominant American culture. Like Malamud's my work seems to find quite naturally a moral center.[6]

Though this moral centre in both the writers seems to have in common a concern for effective acculturation against the "ever present fear of failure and betrayal,"[7] it also shows a divergence in rendering the "schism" in self caused by expatriate identity crisis. In place of Malamud's constant focus on soul searching, Bharati Mukherjee's fictional canvas seems to underscrore a curious guiltlessness consciously mustered as a strategy to survive and to make good. Bharati Mukherjee is concerned about making her picture of Indian life intelligible and interesting to the American readers. But she is too good an artist to distort reality just to capture attention. Avoiding alike stereotyped versions and sentimental exaggerations, she tries to pack into her novels a rich resonance of meaning by the deft device of combining immigrant, feminist and existentialistic perspectives. Instead of writing of backwardness as an area of darkness, she focusses attention on her characters' growing awareness of the dark spots in their lives, and their courageous efforts to discover areas of light. This search for light, for happiness and fulfilment is subtly linked in her fiction to her protagonists' struggle for self-actualization.

The destiny of Jasmine, the protagonist of the novel bearing the same name, best illustrates this. First introduced as the saucy heroine of a short story and later made, with modifications, the protagonist of a frontier novel, Jasmine is not only not prototypically Indian but is shown harbouring a desire for independence and a respect for success that appear incongruous in her Indian setting of poverty, gender-discrimination and rigid social conventions. Jasmine's yearning for these from early childhood marks the beginning of her struggle for self-actualization or the realization or concretization of ardently-cherished ideals. The thrust of my paper is on Jasmine's achieving self-actualization not by a geographical shift to America but by a personality 'honing' through acculturation to different identities she takes on finally to realize that the crux of self-actualization is the exercising of not the Indian or American but the human right to be at peace with herself.

II

Through her innovative technique of alternately highlighting one or the other of the 'mutations' in her heroine's identity—Jyoti, Jasmine, Jase, Jane,—Bharati Mukherjee fills in details about different segments of Jasmine's life in its meandering course through the terrains of Hasnapur, Jullundhur, Florida, Columbia Baden and thence to the road to California. The fragmentation of life suggested by the use of segments in life as plot-nodes acquires additional significance by the dominant narrative voice's underscoring, not a disproportionate importance given to Jasmine when compared to the other characters, but of her total isolation as "a strange pilgrim in an outlandish shrine." Melanie Kaye's comment on this aspect of Bharati Mukherjee's narrative technique merits close scrutiny:

> Mukherjee's particular gift is montage, a jump out movement that creates a bond with the first person narrator and distance from everyone else, thus underscoring with great economy the immigrant's isolation, by-product of American opportunity.[8]

Now for the first phase. Born as Jyoti to a man driven from his affluent house in Lahore to a life of ignominous poverty in the remote Punjab village Hasnapur during the partition riots, Jasmine has early acquaintance with the heart-wrenching agony of people uprooted from their homesteads. Resigned to her supposedly inferior status in society for the sin of being born a girl, and constantly made aware of her misfortune as a dowryless daughter, Jyoti has an uneventful childhood. Two incidents figure prominently in Jasmine's memory of Hasnapur. One is her having had to kill a mad dog rushing to attack her and the other is her receiving a star-like wound on her forehead while she tripped and fell in an attempt to run away from an irate astrologer who predicted an early widowhood for her. The permanent scar left on her forehead by this wound, her third eye as she loved to refer to it, is in a way an indication of the continued hold the astrologer's words exercise on her even after her breaking away from Indian roots and settling in the USA. Her wanting to learn English is dimly perceived by everyone as her "wanting the world." (68)

Marriage to Prakash brings about a total change in her mindset. The 'newness' of life in Jullundhur, beginning with the change of her name to Jasmine, makes her realize that 'motherhood' need not be her sole destiny. Enthused by Prakash's plans of eventually settling into a much better life-style in America with their own business concern, she starts assisting him in the repair of electronic goods by way of supplementing their meagre income.

Prakash's untimely death at the hands of fundamentalists—the self-styled "Khalsa lions" spreading terror in the region by their acts of senseless violence—leaves her grief-stricken and frustrated with ineffectual anger. Rebelling against the idea of spending the rest of her life as a destitute widow at Hasnapur, she prevails on her brothers to arrange for her transport to America on a forged passport; her plan of committing 'suttee' after reaching the campus where Prakash wanted to enroll is a gesture of protest, a despairing girl's desperate bid to 'do' something to express her anger at Fate's cruel thwarting of her husband's diasporal dreams. If it is just a giving up on life, she could have committed suicide in Hasnapur itself. Her intense nature demanded idealistic expression and at this stage in her life, 'suttee' was the only sublime action she could think of. The daring of the young rustic girl in undertaking this hazardous trip abroad is a measure of her innate affinity to the American ideal of fearless enterprise. Jasmine's image seems to be a personification of Bharati Mukherjee's concept of Americanness as an outlook on life. As cited by Davidar, "Some people were meant to be American even if they never leave their village in Punjab. At heart they are

American. It is a desire for more, more, more."[9]

The desire to hold her own against the blind forces of destiny urges her to leave India, but unfortunately her American experience begins on a jarring note—her brutal rape by the deformed captain half-face, in whose ship she is smuggled into America. The dismal view of the Florida swamps that she gets on her first entry into America, "Eden's waste: plastic bottles, floating oranges, boards, sodden boxes, white and green plastic sacks tied shut but picked open by birds and pulled apart by crabs," (107) seems to be an appropriate backdrop to the horrible fate awaiting her. Incensed by the outrage she becomes a veritable "Kali," knifes him to death, sets the building on fire and walks out, distraught, dead tired, with no destination in mind. When she falls down, nearly dead out of shock, starvation and fatigue, Mrs. Lillian Gordon enters into her life like a deus ex machina. Her hospitality and her advice, "Let the past make you wary, by all means. But do not let it deform you" (131) help her recoup physically and mentally and with her help she sets out to meet Professor Vadhera, the gentleman who was instrumental in Prakash's securing admission in an engineering course. Dejected by the discovery that the Professor is eking out a living not by teaching but by trading in human hair, and irked by the diligently-guarded 'ethnicity' in that household including the austerities of widowhood she is expected to observe, she decides to leave that house. Prakash's struggle to make something more of his life than fate intended (85) and her own ardent desire, "If we could just get away from India then all fates would be cancelled. We'd start with new fates new stars. We could say or be anything we wanted. We'd be on the otherside of earth, out of God's sight," (89) is too deeply etched on Jasmine's mind to allow her to agree to getting engulfed by insularity and she leaves the place determined to live on her own. This move is itself an indication that self-actualization is already taking shape in her life and it was made possible by acculturation to the American way of thinking along with the American way of dressing. With the actualization of the desire for independence the door is shut to the passive resignation extolled by her grandmother since individual effort means nothing." (57) It should be noted here that Jasmine's protest, like that of Bharati Mukherjee herself, is not against Indian culture *per se* but against its 'retentiveness,' its "particular way of partially comprehending the world."[10] After a short period of hand-to-mouth existence Jasmine gets the chance to work as 'caregiver' to Duff, the little daughter of Wylie and Taylor. Jasmine enjoys her new financial independence as well as the affectionate treatment she is shown by her employers, Taylor in particular. Wylie's falling out of love with Taylor and her decision to live with another man shocks Jasmine at first. But soon, a bond of intimacy develops between her and Taylor.

Jasmine's calm acceptance of both – the change in her own scale of values and the largesse of Taylor in remaining above racial and cultural barriers – is worth-noting:

> Taylor didn't want to change me. He didn't want to scour and sanitize the foreignness. . . . I changed because I wanted to. To bunker oneself inside nostalgia to sheath the heart in a bullet-proof vest, was to be a coward. On Claremont Avenue, in the Hayeses' big, clean, brightly lit apartment I bloomed from a different alien with forged documents into adventurous Jase. (185)

This idyllic life comes to a sudden halt when her accidental sighting of Sukha, the terrorist who killed her husband makes her flee from that place. Her main reason for running away is the fear that her presence in their household may jeopardize the safety of Taylor and Duff.

While in Iowa, a providential meeting with Mrs. Ripplemeyer, whose kind offer of finding employment for Jane in the bank owned by her son, ends in Bud's falling in love with her. Bharati Mukherjee's use of friendly souls readily giving advice and assistance has to be understood as a tribute she wants to pay to American generosity rather than as a flawed narrative device. As she says: "My characters are survivors. They have been helped as I have, by good strong people of conviction."

Jane settles down to a peaceful life in Bud's house, happy in her new financial security and her new stepmother status with regard to Du, a sixteen-year old Vietnam war victim adopted by Bud, after his grown-up sons left the house and he is separated from his wife Karin. Violence mars the even tenor of her life yet again, this time in Bud's becoming a cripple waist downwards by a disgruntled farmer's shooting at him from point blank range. It is not just Bud, but the entire countryside, the very serenity of rural life that is the victim here as it was in Punjab at the hands of terrorist violence. Sarah Curtis rightly notes:

> What makes Iowa similar to the Punjab is not just that "Nothing is fair. God is cruel" (Mata jee's cry) but that existence in both places is frequently interrupted and constantly shattered by violence. The most terrifying aspect of the violence is that its roots are comprehensible but it strikes at random.[11]

Feeling miserable thinking that if Karin were on the scene she would have somehow averted the disaster, she exerts herself to the utmost in seeing to it that Bud is comfortable. Her patience mollifies even Karin who was till then infuriated by the news of Jasmine's pregnancy by Bud. The valuable lesson she has already learned, that in "America nothing lasts – Nothing is forever, nothing is so terrible or wonderful that it won't disintegrate," (181) fortifies her in warding off guilt feelings about usurping Karin's place in Bud's heart. She has learned to adjust to a new set of values but she has definitely not shed all values altogether. Her analysis of her relationship with Bud shows that there is a clear distinction in her mind between living with someone separated from his wife and deliberately breaking up a home: "Bud would have left Karin or twisted in mid life until he dropped. I was a catalyst. Not a cuase." (200)

A sudden letter from Taylor informing her that he and Duff would be calling on her shortly comes as a pleasant surprise. Du's cool announcement of his decision to go to California and stay with his sister and her family makes her worry about its probable impact on Bud. An exile herself she fully understands Du's need to 'belong' and silently watches him leave and breaks the news to Bud as gently as she can.

She rebuffs the overtures of love made by young Darrel, their next-door neighbour and feels sorry for him for being tied down to farm work tending pigs, while his heart was set on going to some big city and get rich the easy way. His suicide shatters her and Bud's plans to legalize their relationship by marriage adds to her gloom.

Taylor's arrival at this juncture is a welcome relief to her and when he in his winning way convinces her that there is nothing wrong in her leaving Bud, she feels reassured and consents to go with him and Duff to the west coast, may be California, "greedy with wants and reckless from hopes." (241)

Jasmine's walking out of Bud's life is not a wanton act of frivolity. Her two remarks, "The moment I have dreamed a thousand times finally arrives" (237) and "I am not choosing between two men. I am caught between the promise of America and old-world dutifulness," (240) clarify for us that it was not a rash abandonment of responsibilities. In a way this decision of Jasmine is a resonant response to the courage she admired in Du in trying to take charge of his life, and the cowardice of Darrel in trying to run away from the problems of life by the extreme step of death. Her desire for self actualization – "I want to do the right thing. I don't want to be a terrible person" (239) – has nothing to do with guilt associated with 'sin.' Jasmine's lack of guilt proves not her 'callousness' but her conscious striving to do only what she thinks is right. Karin is aware of this, hence her statement earlier in the novel: "This is Puritan country. We are born with guilt or quickly learn it. Guilt twists a person." (228)

Her sense of 'relief' at leaving Bud rather than guilt underscores that she was happy to be doing what she had been wishing to do from a long time back, a wish strengthened by her sincere concern that the astrologer's prediction should not take a toll of Bud's life. Jasmine's linking her life to that of Taylor is to be seen as a validation of her avowed belief, "Treat every second of your existence as a possible assignment from God," (61) a reaffirmation of the courage she mustered in killing the mad dog saying "I was not ready to die." (56)

Jasmine may or may not appear as a 'rabblemaker' by everyone stepping into the orbit of her life, but at every stage in her trouble-torn life, in all her identities as Jyoti, Jasmine, Jase and Jane, she seems to act boldly and unhesitatingly, thrilled at the prospect of 'adventure, risk, transformation.' (241)

The word 'transformation' together with her words of farewell to the mental image of the astrologer which has been haunting her all these years, "Watch me reposition the stars," suggest that Jasmine has indeed achieved self-actualization in America – the only land on earth that gives one ample opportunity to work at making a dream a reality.

Thus synchronous with her self-actualization Jasmine becomes truly Americanized, not just in peripheral social or cultural mores but in a primal "intensity of spirit," and finds peace neither in India, nor America, but in the 'American dream.'

NOTES

1. Sybil Steinberg, "*PW* Interviews," *Publishers Weekly*, 25 Aug. 1989, p. 47.
2. Bharati Mukherjee, "Introduction," *Darkness* (Ontario: Penguin, 1986), p. 2.
3. *Ibid.*, p. 1.
4. *Ibid.*, p. 3.
5. Steinberg, p. 47.
6. Alison B. Carb, "An Interview with Bharati Mukherjee," *The Massachusetts Review*, Winter 1988, p. 650.
7. *Darkness*, p. 2.
8. Melanie Kaye, Review of *Jasmine*, *Women's Review of Books*, April 1990, p. 7.
9. David Davidar, "The Immigrant Native," *The Indian Express*, Feb. 19, 1989, p. 5.
10. *Darkness*, p. 3.

Jasmine: An Odyssey of Unhousement and Enhousement[1]

S. INDIRA

"I'm writing about the here and now of America"[2] says Bharati Mukherjee, claiming herself to be not just an expatriate novelist but a mainstream American writer. Her immigration to the United States is to her "a movement away from the aloofness of expatriation to the exuberance of immigration."[3] Her Canadian experience as an expatriate who was being constantly crippled in self-defence in a hostile environment has made her welcome the freedom of the anonymous in the U.S. Unlike other Indian writers such as Kamala Markandaya and Anita Desai who treated the Indian immigrant situation as one of conflict and adjustment with a little understanding and love, Bharati Mukherjee gives it a new, challenging perspective enabling the immigrants to emerge out of their cocoons of defence into the openness of assertion and say that they do belong.

Jasmine, the fascinating heroine of her third novel, stands as an example of the "fusion" the author claims is occurring now: "immigration was a two-way process and both the whites and immigrants were growing into a third thing by this interchange and experience."[4] While Tara and Dimple, the protagonists of *The Tiger's Daughter* and *Wife* become isolated, rootless aliens because of their ambivalent attitude to their native tradition as well as the culture of the new world, Jasmine enjoys the assimilated status of immigration by a sheer will to bond herself to her adopted land.

Jasmine, whose maiden name was Jyoti, is up against fate from an age as early as seven years. Born in Hasnapur, a small village in Punjab, she did not feel cowed down by the prediction of her widowhood and exile. The 'scar' on her forehead is "a third eye" (5) to her. Raging against fate and the norms of society which tried to condition her existence, Jasmine asserts that she is not just nothing.

Driven by a need of power, she kills a mad dog, refuses to marry anyone who doesn't speak English as "to want English" is to "want the world." (68) Marrying Prakash, a young engineer, who too is obsessed like her "to make something more of his life than fate intended," (85) Jyoti begins the journey of realizing her 'self' and 'potential.'

Renamed as Jasmine, joyously sharing the ambition of her husband, she looks forward to going to America, a land of opportunities. Even when this dream gets shattered by the murder of Prakash on the eve of his departure, Jasmine does not regress into being Jyoti again. She does not shuttle between identities; instead, she decides to go to America and thus fulfil Prakash's mission and perform 'sati' on the grounds of the university where he gained admission to study. But once landed in America, her old-self strongly conditioned by the society into which she is born, gives birth to a new, exuberent self that denies death and welcomes the prospect of a different life. Given a new insight into life by Lillian Gordon's most practical and humanist approach that made life possible for anyone, Jasmine goes to New York. But, to her horror, she finds New York to be an "archipelago of Ghettoes seething with aliens." (140) Unlike Vadheras who have retired behind the ghetto walls and the "fortress of Punjabiness," (148) Jasmine longs to explore the new land which intrigues her. She wants to distance itself from everything Indian, everything Jyoti-like. Having learned to "walk and talk" American, she grabs every opportunity to become American and to prove to the world what "a girl from a swampy backwater could accomplish." (160) As Duff's day mummy and Taylor and Wylie's au pair in Manhattan, Jasmine becomes Jase, which marks the beginning of her acculturation. Eagerly responding to the warmth of friendliness shown by Wylie and Taylor who called her their "caregiver" but not a "maid servant," working at part-time jobs like answering phones and tutoring graduate students in Punjabi at the University and absorbing the alien culture rather greedily, Jasmine gains a personality and becomes a confident individual. The transformation is quite fast but she is unable to slow down the pace as she is unwilling to abandon the ride she is on. Pulling herself out of her native culture is painful but exhilarating at the same time as she feels it is cowardly to "bunker oneself inside nostalgia." (185) With the healing touch of people like Lillian Gordon, Kate and Taylor, who treated her as an intelligent, refined, sincere and affectionate person, Jasmine blooms from being a diffident alien with forged documents into adventurous Jase, living only for the present. The tugging between the opposing forces does not intimidate her, rather it excites her. Amidst the other immigrant domestics who hang suspended between the two worlds, Jasmine feels proud that she is getting rooted in the new world.

While America taught her to live with ease and confidence despite her fluid identity and undocumented status, Jasmine gave her care, concern and love to those who believed her and who needed her. Taylor accepts her for what she is: he is neither condescending in his kindness nor uneasy because she is an illegal immigrant from a backward country. He confesses his love for her and his emotional need of her after Wylie deserts him. Touched by his sincerity and genuineness, Jasmine feels drawn to him. Her immigrant status does in no way obstruct the emotional rapport between them.

Another eventful chapter begins in Jasmine's chequered life when she leaves Taylor and Duff fearing their safety because of the hovering presence of death in the form of Sukhawinder, the Khalsa Lion who killed Prakash in India. A chance meeting with another saving angel, mother Ripplemeyer, a job in Iowa's bank and a place in the banker Bud Ripplemeyer's heart and home are more than anything Jasmine has bargained for. Her foreignness fascinates the fifty-year-old Bud who looks upon her as an inscrutable mystery and feels rejuvenated by her Eastern vitality and wisdom. Assuming a new identity to fit her role as Bud's wife (though she has not actually married him) Jasmine becomes "Jane." She looks upon herself a catalyst and not the cause to bring about the divorce of Bud and Karin in mid-life. For all America gave her, Jasmine paid back with gratitude and love. She serves Bud patiently and fondly after he was crippled. With her kind composure, she makes Karin understand that she is not her enemy and it's Bud's happiness that matters to both of them. She finds herself thoroughly welcome in the home and society of mother Ripplemeyer and longs to belong to that tribe which represented the best in America. Sought after by a University Professor who wanted to share her out-of-body experiences with her, Jasmine couldn't help but marvelling at America's elasticity that can make a sixth-class drop-out from an Indian village to be a fit companion to scholarly people. Touched by the American need to make intuition tangible and the belief in Eastern mysticism, she comforts Dr. Mary Webb that she certainly empathizes with her soul's mutable genetic journey, having travelled in time and space herself.

To change from Jyoti to Jasmine, Jasmine to Jase, and Jase to Jane is not an easy process. She survived hideous times that involved rapes and murders, terrifying challenges and unimaginable crises. She is not sentimental about her Indian identity, nor does she suffer from nostalgic longing. Instead, she has used all her strength and resolve to forge new alliances in the friendly soil of the adopted homeland. The 'fusion' between the East and West pleases her and she rejoices that her journey to America has unfolded her "affirming" self.

While Jasmine is triumphant that her transformation has been genetic, Du, her adopted son remains a defiant immigrant who refuses to assimilate. Unlike her, he has tried to develop contacts with the other Vietnamese in Baden and maintain his hyphenated identity, Vietnamese-American. In spite of his brilliant performance at school and his genius for adaptation and appropriation of technology, Du can never be a total American as he would always be attached to an experience, an American father like Bud could not fathom. When Jasmine admits that for some immigrants there is no way except that, Bud says, "But not for you, Jane, that's what I love about you." (232) It is perhaps this Americanness in her that has made Jasmine accept Taylor's offer to go to West towards an unknown future, yet another adventure leaving the security of Bud's home. As an Indian girl, she would not have dreamt of deserting Bud, denying him even his child. Having seen death and the worst of life closely many a time, having suffered and survived several times, she seems to regard her relationship with Bud just another phase in her journey of self. It is America once again that has taught her that nothing lasts in that country. "Nothing is forever, nothing is so terrible, or so wonderful, that it won't disintegrate." (181)

Bharati Mukherjee admits in an interview that her characters are a breed of pioneers who have the guts to forsake a predictable life in order to throw themselves into a new one.[5] In *Jasmine*, she celebrates both the undaunted spirit and enthusiasm of a village girl who blossomed out of a bruised past into a challenging personality and a complete individual and the status of immigration in the U.S., which facilitates aliens not only to be acculturated but also to be assimilated into their adopted land.

NOTES

1. The phrase is used by Clark Blaise in his book *Resident Alien* and referred to in the interview by N.P. Krishna Kumar.
2. N.P. Krishna Kumar, "India is in touch with us," interview with Bharati Mukherjee and Clark Blaise, *The Indian Express Sunday Magazine*, September 13, 1992, p. 6.
3. Bharati Mukherjee, "Introduction" to *Darkness* (India: Penguin Books, 1990), p. 3.
4. Interview in *The Hindustan Times*, February 9, 1990, p. 3.
5. Interview in *The Indian Express Sunday Magazine*.

Expatriate Experience in Farhana Sheikh's *The Red Box*

F.A. INAMDAR

Carol P. Christ tells us what distinctive trend is followed in women's fiction:

> Women's social quest concerns women's struggle to gain respect, equality and freedom in society . . . spiritual quest concerns a woman's awakening to the depths of her soul . . . provides orientation for women's social quest and grounds it in something larger than individual or even collective achievements . . . supports her when her own personal determination falters.[1]

The Red Box evokes social and spiritual quest of not only mothers and daughters from Pakistan but of fathers and sons. In the novel, Raisa was born in Pakistan but grew up in "the heady London of the 1960's" as the blurb of the book puts it. While she is "researching problems of identity for Asian girls," she not only discovers their lives but also comes to recognize her own life. Tahira and Nasreen are fifteen-year olds studying at South Park School. Raisa interviews them, in the process she is being pulled into their lives. She has a close look at Tahira's mother's life, i.e. Nargis and Nasreen's i.e., Mrs. Ehsan's. While Raisa has no mother, Tahira's mother is a divorcee. Though Raisa comes from a wealthy family with a barrister father, yet her mother died working in a factory to make both ends meet. Nasreen's father studied engineering at London University for a year. he gave up his studies, as he had to work to live. He works as a bus conductor and will lose his job soon because he is over forty. To this search for a comfortable home there is the problem of exploitation of the employer. Added to these are the psychological tensions of daughters who have kicked the heels to join the western mode of life, who are in a hurry to lose their virginity and the parents who are nervous about whether they would save their face in their biradari i.e. in their social circle. To these aspects are added the portraits of immigrants on their brief visits to their native land. Against this domestic drama there is the big cultural divide not only in society but at school. My aim in this paper is to deal with these thematic problems in the novel to see how the expatriate experience is central to the novel.

I

Raisa's grandfather's home is an Eden. She is forced to accompany her mother to London at a tender age of seven. To Raisa like immigrants, London is much like Hell. This is prefiguratively conveyed through the child's reluctance to come down from the first floor. She is tempted metaphorically to come down with baits. It is like Satan tempting Eve with the forbidden fruit: "huge boxes of the sweetest chocolates and platefuls of the most piquant tamarind if only she could come down."[2] Raisa at school experiences racial discrimination when she hammers her fist into Judy Butlin's face: "You fucking half-breed, go back to your mud hut!" (193) She could not defend her Asian friend Rezuana when Lee Rollings ridiculed her by saying "She bathed in curry." (194) Raisa, during her school days takes to dancing and visits Roundhouse. "It was a place where a boy smoked pot, drank alcohol, took off his clothes and danced naked for all to see?" (198) In that place she is tempted to fall in love with Alex Brown: "I wanted him to want me. . . . I saw myself as he saw me: desirable, beautiful, sensual." (200)

When her mother returns from Pakistan after her grandfather's death, Raisa's avaaragardi, this gallivanating is checked. But yet she feels fascinated by Eric, a Denmark boy of twenty. Her mother takes it out on her father for making his daughter English. The Western mode has gone to Raisa's head. She writes about her mother when the latter stops her from going out: "I hate her, I hate the bitch! I hope she gets killed!" This is the greatest fall that Raisa as an immigrant suffers. She has no regards for her mother. Her mind is full of "crashing music and the dancing in the magic shade and light" and her body melting into Eric. (211)

Raisa's mother's importance dawns upon her only when she is

dead. She searches for her mother's smell in her mother's dresses: "I felt sick and I missed her." (221) Through the red box deeply hidden in her mother's clothes, Raisa comes to know her mother's life. She had worked in a factory under pseudo name, once as 'Sony' the next as 'Sunaya.' The factory people wanted her to work harder. If she had lived long enough, they would have sacked her. (224) Hence, father let her suffer that strain and humiliation and her brothers had been greedy denying share in her father's property. Raisa realizes: "sitting in front of my mother's suitcase, injustice and my own life became linked." (226)

Raisa's father helps her in her spiritual quest. It is bound up with a woman's respect in society and her status in her family. If a girl mixes with boys and has sexual relations, it is the ultimate transgression. Of course, there is the freedom to socialize on professional and educational level. But the physical surrender of a male to a female is defilement. The Pakistan immigrants manage to steer clear of the loose and licentious western mode of life. Raisa's mother lived by her izzat. For her mother sexual transgression was a cardinal crime, worse than taking of a life. It was not only the defilement of the body but of the soul. For her once a man or woman lets slip—the person becomes guilty. You can try to wash away guilt in life but then you have to twist and turn and distort the natural flow of morality. Those who respect human life, can't pursue sexual adventures. Your love for your children is based on the sanctity of sexual decency.

The novelist presents antithetical lives of the immigrants. Tahira and Nasreen are London born. The girls' outlook on life is strongly rooted in the attitude of their mothers. Tahira has no father. It is too much for her mother to handle a job outside and the domestic responsibility. With this background Tahira wants to go totally English. But she is torn between the pulls of religious restrictions and the freedom of the West. She succumbs to the western influence in the early part of her school life to the extent of losing her virginity to Arif, a Pakistani.

She goes through hellish conflict in her mind while Arif holds out threats of blackmail and wants her to meet him everyday after school hours. He even phones her younger sister to find out Tahira's whereabouts. The novelist has been successful in evoking Tahira fighting a lone battle of moral and spiritual responsibility and, finally, deciding for herself how best to shape her life. This is done only because Tahira is a precocious girl thinking independently for herself.

She decides to meet Arif in a hotel and thrashes him for his womanizing tendencies:

> I ain't scared of you. You can't bloody touch me. (169)
>
> I might just have told my lot that you forced me – you know, like raped me. (170)

She further adds: "what are you really? Just a poor little Paki who helps his dad on his little stall shop." Then she holds him down with her moral angle:

> You wouldn't like no one treating your sister like that. . . . You wouldn't want no bloke to be with your sister as you was with me, would ya? Answer me that? (172)

Tahira could handle that Arif, the devil because she has a strong religious background, inculcated by her mother.

Whenever Tahira accompanied her mother, the latter wanted her to put on Shalwaar Kameez and to put her dupatta on. (13) Tahira has her own devilish pranks of going to disco parties without letting her mother know about them. She has her own insular restrictions of not drinking, smoking and dancing with boys because "it is not o.k." (21) Naturally, she does not like the ways of the English girls of "having kids . . . when they're not even married." (22)

While there is a complex dimension to Tahira's portrait, Nasreen's is evoked totally on traditional background. For her marrying within their own religious group is ensuring a strong and stable marriage. She brings out why the intercaste marriages fall apart. They go to discos. They see other boys and get inclined to leave their husbands. On the contrary Muslim women cover their whole bodies so that men cannot notice their beauty. Their men are also faithful to the wedlock. Her views cannot stand the test of the common human experience of Muslim men. They are notorious for their search for new pastures. Moreover, the novel itself does not present the picture of such a couple. Raisa's mother goes out to work in the English dress and yet remains loyal to her husband. And the barrister is faithful to his wife even after her death for his strong moral and spiritual views.

These two girls experience threat to their status even when they walk along London streets. A group of youths pass filthy remarks:

"dirty paki glags" (53) though they shout back insults at them: "white trashm pig, bastards!" (53) This incident reminds us of Bharati Mukherjee's *The Tiger's Daughter* where Tara has to deal with violence and ghettos in American life. Similarly we remember the immigrant experience of Sarah in Anita Desai's *Bye-Bye Blackbird* when the boys shout at her: "Hurry, hurry, Mrs. Curry!"[3]

The feminine perspective comes through Raisa's interview of Tahira and Nasreen. For Nasreen the natural woman is one who gives birth and looks after the family. Only women have children. For Tahira women can be lots of other things – doctors, lawyers. She does not want to have children and does not want to cook and clean for them. For Tahira woman can do different things. According to Nasreen they can be really them when they are at home with their family. But when they are with friends, they put up their false selves. Their friends support their lies. While they tell their parents that they are going on a school trip, but in fact staying at a friend's house and pretending they were grown up and having a nice time is bad for her. It involves lies. Her part with the friends was she as well, but that was a bad part of her because she felt guilty. The aspect of the problem is seen differently by Tahira. If she does not go with her friends, she will be out of the circle when they are all together. This is the way to meet new people, and friends form a part of your education – social life lived on your own. While these adolescents are busy sorting out things for themselves, their mothers are caught up with different perspectives. Nasreen's mother Mrs. Ehsan works from home, stitching blouses. London is not her country. She intends to go back home "when we have enough money." (45) She knows that the English hate them: "This isn't our country – they think we shouldn't be here." (122) She can't even allow her child to play in the street: "'What a land we have come to' the woman sighed . . . 'Hai, when I think of that woman whose son was killed in that school. . . .Tell Babu to come in now.'" (24) Like Tahira, her mother Nargis has complex problems to face. Her problems of identity and culture are: "who we are – how we live – what we suffer, how we fight back." (142) She does not want her children to work in the places she works. She aims at their better life. To develop their own way of living in England different from the English. For that, education is very important. She is a divorcee. She works at K & K fashions. As she is not formally educated, her employer, Mr. Khan holds out threats of dismissal. She does not know how they had to be registered, without that they can't claim benefits such as sickness, unemployment. Nor does she know the new immigration laws. She is a bold woman like her daughter. Therefore, she is hectoring the others. She was not ready to accept things that were not light. She had not accepted her things in marriage and, she thinks that she should not in her work. One sadly expects that the novelist would have made Raisa help these helpless solve their problems with her laudable aims such as: "unless we understand who we are – how we live, what we suffer, what we admire, what we hate, what we put up with. What we fight for – and how we have become who we are . . . how will we ever change the things that hold us down?" (155) For Nargis things do not change. Her worries crop up for the safety of her daughter:

> Had the grey car stopped for Tahira? . . . More and more her life had become an endless chaos of worries. As soon as one was temporarily put to rest, another came forward to drain her energy and deny her peace of mind. (159)

This is an adequate evocation of the immigrant abroad in general and the modern man in particular.

These very immigrants when they come back home for a brief stay show off themselves as if they have dropped from heaven with their attempts to build an atmosphere of London and New York clubs with scotches and mint Juleps. The novel adequately represents the life of Ali with Zeenat. How Zeenat, when she went off to study in the states was caught with some American. (25) Marium is another such immigrant. Her breath smells of tobacco and alcohol. She is slurred of speech and flushed of face. (25) Soraya is a girl who hardly smoked in London, but in Pakistan becomes a chain smoker. Some of these men from abroad drive away as heroes in Hollywood or Indian movies: "the wind blowing through their laughter and hair . . . Yusuf with his cartier watch, cigarette in mouth and single hand driving . . . the heroes of a celluloid fantasy." (26)

II

A big cultural divide is represented by the fissure in the black and the white in the South Park School. Jamshid is insulted by the white girls crowding round his table in the dining hall. In his heart of hearts he thinks: "Do you know how much I hate them, hate them, for their filthy language and their filthy hate of me." (9) The fourth years have threatened the first years. Their dad has stood laughing when they threw stones at the blacks. In the dining room, one of the girls, taunts Jamshid: "Look, you bloody wog, this ain't your country, this ain't your school. 'They've got no rights!'" (10) To spill salt on his wound they sit at his table and refer to the girls from Pakis that they are not capable of having big pricks. This makes Jamshid lose control over himself. He calls the white girls prostitutes. This results in a shower of blows by the white girls on Jamshid. He thinks it was the mark of weakness. He hated everything: the girls, the school, the country, and his family who did not fight back. (11) The Muslim girls debate as passive spectators whether it is right on Jamshid's part to call the white girls prostitutes. They think how the English teachers do not take action against the white boys when they call the black girls "slags." (52) And the Muslim London-born girls think that it is their own country as they pay "taxes." (57) These girls are afraid of the white boys because if they wear Shalwaar Kameez they taunt that they have "night clothes on." (14) The white teachers punish these girls if they tell the facts. Tahira got a slap on her face for calling "the deputy head as a racialist." (14) They are all filled with shame because they can't help themselves. They cannot defend themselves. (15) The teachers did nothing when all the Asian students were locked up by the white students. The Asian girls have lost faith in the teachers. They do not want to open up before them for fear of being trapped. They bitterly remember how Kassim's family was burnt alive and another Asian student's house was set on fire. They know for certain that had that been a white man's house, "they would have caught some one quick." (17) Even Tahira's mother was spat at when she was coming home all tired. (17) The Asian girls can't report the insults on them because the teachers would not believe them. Mr. Kern, the headmaster expels Mr. Jamshid on the ground that he had a knife on him during the quarrel though Terry is left scot-free even though he possessed one at the time. The words of Jamshid fall on deaf ears: "Amer and his friends carry knives, so do Amer's family . . they throw stones at us in the park, come down streets with knives and poles and throw things down letter boxes." (76) To these complaints the headmaster's classic reply is: Such a case is for the police to look into. The Asian's self-defence is taken for violence and is considered a criminal activity. (90)

In London the novelist evokes a common destiny for the Asians.

they stand together in their hours of crisis. This is noticed by the English children: "one of them gets it, and they all gang up together. Makes you sick." (118) When Tahira sees Gita in the distance and runs towards her. (189) In this, we the bums in India have a message for us. Our politicians kill us for their crown. We will learn to live as one only when Tahira in Asia runs for Gita.

III

The immigration problem in *The Red Box* has a rare focus when compared with Bharati Mukherjee's *The Tiger's Daughter.* In Mukherjee's novel Tara's immigration problem is marginal. In *The Red Box* it is all-pervading. You have it while coming back home dog tired from your job. Your children have it in school. You have it in factory and in the street out there. The red box is an image of Raisa's mother's plight sacrificing her dignity of mind and her love of home and hearth at the behest of her husband's ordres: "wearing the skirt, being pushed to becoming somebody that she hides her woes in that box. The wage slip in the box reveals her loss of identity: "My mother had worked in a factory where one week they thought she was 'Sony' and the next 'Sunaya.'" (224) Her mother's brothers were as much to be blamed for the agony of Raisa's mother as her husband and the daughter.

The red box extends into a symbol in evoking a current of humiliation spreading from the beginning of the novel till the end. Tahira's mother, Nargis is in search of her own identity when she loses the "connectedness" with her husband, she is a victim of dependent personality disorder unable to bring to book her exploiting employer. On the contrary, Tahira is in search of becoming a wife and mother and using these as source of strength to create an enlarged vision of the expatriate predicament. Her struggle is for keeping alive her British nationality and her own self respect and the prospects of a successful career woman. But her aims are thwarted by the natives. Hence it is a red box in her life that might endanger her future endeavours. Nasreen and her mother, Mrs. Ehsan are always under the shadow of the red box. Their lives are beset with dangers day in and day out.

The symbol of the red box extends into the lives of the Asian school children. They are subjected to untold humiliations by not only the school authorities but also the natives around them.

NOTES

1. Charlone Spretnak, ed., *The Politics of Women's Spirituality* (New York: Doubleday, 1982), p. 328
2. Farhana Sheikh, *The Red Box* (Calcutta: Rupa, 1991), p. 1.
3. Anita Desai, *Bye-Bye, Blackbird* (Delhi: Hind, 1971), p. 37.

George Lamming and the Caribbean Experience of Expatriation

C. VIJAYASREE

Expatriation on a large scale constitutes one of the most significant historical developments in all post-colonial societies. In fact it has the quality of intuitive migration of lemmings and cuckoos in winter. The mass expatriation of intellectuals from the post-colonial societies in the fifties and sixties is symptomatic of a violent social change taking place in these communities beginning with colonization, and gaining momentum in the first half of this century. Emigration becomes an important trope in the post-colonial discourse because it not only constitutes the commonly-shared experience of these peoples, but also emerges the lived experience of their writers. While expatriation appears as a recurring motif in new literatures across cultures, responses to this experience seem to be culture-specific. Within a culture there are individual variations, which do fall into certain discernible patterns. For instance, in most Indian writers expatriation leads to a sense of calm resignation and realization: "Home is the place/where we gather grace." In the African context, home-coming is wrought with more intense psychological problems. The Caribbean experience of expatriation is much more agonizing since Caribbeans as a community are essentially "settlers" severed from their respective cultures and deposited on an alien soil as a part of the European scramble for power. Their attempts at making homes in the new-found land are frustrated by the constant interference of colonial domination and authority. Against this background of a sense of original isolation, expatriation is nothing but a flight from a scene of spiritual sterility, cultural void and emotional deprivation. Expatriation becomes analogous to self-imposed exile and constitutes a part of West Indian quest for identity.

Furthermore, expatriation acquires specific pertinence in any serious study of Caribbean literature, because majority of their writers moved out of their homes in different directions – USA, Canada and Britain – all in search of "a better break." Much of what constitutes Caribbean literature is written outside the islands. The blossoming of the literary talent in the fifties which produced such writers as Wilson Harris, Samuel Selvon, Derek Walcott, V.S. Naipaul and George Lamming saw them all become exiles because they chose to flee the society that was stifling their creativity. They were compelled to leave because they knew they had no relevance in countries which had no use for arts or literature. Large-scale exportation of Caribbean writing talent that began in the fifties goes on until present day and a whole new generation of Caribbean writers including David Dabydeen, Joan Riley, Caryl Philips have set up homes in Britain. All these writers, however, cling to their roots and show varying degrees of attachment to the West Indies from where they draw their sustenance. Much of Caribbean writing is thus born out of this tension of trying to inhabit two worlds at once and reflects these writers' struggle to cope with the demands of expatriate existence. Lamming's fictional work best represents this tension and this struggle in all its ramifications.

Expatriation is the lived experience of his life and *leitmotif* of his creative work as well. Born in 1927, Lamming was a young man in the forties, "a period of almost permanent revolution"[1] as Lamming himself describes it. His childhood and adolescence in Barbados actually parallel the development of a new historical epoch in the Caribbean. In 1947 he went to Trinidad where he had a consciousness-rousing involvement with a group of aspiring Trinidadian writers including Clifford Sealy and Cecil Herbert. Lamming left for England at 23, and his departure was a part of a major socio-political movement in the Caribbean. For the next thirty years Lamming remained largely a resident in England and USA, yet never losing his contact with the Caribbean. He always stayed close to developments at home and all his six novels written and published outside Barbados have for their central concern Caribbean experience, and record with barometric sensitivity the changes occurring in the socio-political life in the islands over a period of three decades. How does the physical distancing and alienation effect his ideological and artistic vision? How does expatriation as a condition of everyday existence influence a writer's creative imagination and vocation?

Expatriation is a recurring thematic motif in Lamming's fiction, and in fact it may be taken to be a sort of thematic link connecting his novels. His first novel, *In the Castle of My Skin* (1953), mixes autobiography and fiction to recreate the political ethos of the Caribbean in the thirties and forties. While the focus is primarily on the collapse of rural structures, emigration is an important secondary theme. In a West Indian village caught in a political turmoil as a consequence of colonial exploitation, it is Trumper, the blackboy who returns after a sojourn in America that clearly perceives the power game being played by colonial landlords and their local stooges. He also brings to the apathetic masses, the message of black brotherhood. He develops racial consciousness when he leaves the obscuring intimacy of the island and enters the impersonal larger world of America. Lamming describes this new awareness in the black boy as follows:

> He was a negro and he was proud. Now he would walk in the sun or stand on the higher hill and proclaim himself the blackest evidence of the whiteman's denial of consciousness.[2]

Trumper's response actually echoes Lamming's own experience as an expatriate in London: "When I was writing *In the Castle of My Skin* what happened was that I had become aware of Africa in the flesh. The first time I met Africans was in London and I think there was a lot of influence there."[3] In the Caribbean context, a journey away from self begins on the island itself. It is triggered by the experience of being a colonial in whose imagination education and religion foster a myth of economic and cultural dependence of Little England on Mother Country. Expatriation, as Lamming suggests at this stage, becomes a social, political and psychological necessity in a situation where an individual has lost touch with the historical and political forces that shape his country. As Ngugi rightly points out, it is "the symbol of a struggling West Indian alienated from his past and the immediate world."[4]

The Emigrants (1954), Lamming's second novel, focusses on the mass exodus of the West Indians to Great Britain following the Second World War. The passengers that board the ship represent a microcosm of the West Indian world which splinters on arrival in London. They all seem to be in a flight, a flight from the restrictions and humiliations of the island life and their journey reenacts the middle passage theme of displacement. As Jamaican, one of the passengers on board, says: "West Indies people, whatever island you bring them from, them want to prove something." He adds:

> Them all want to prove something and them sensitive, them sensitive, them fraid, cause them ain't want the foreign man to feel them ain't provin.[5]

What motivates their pathetic flight to the distant unknown lands is "a psychology of expectations whose melancholy rewards had to be sought outside."[6]

Of the several emigrants that reach England, none really succeeds. Some are total failures; many wear out in the struggle; most of them end up as schizophrenic personalities, living corpses. Having advocated emigration as the only solution for the Caribbean socio-political impasse, why does the writer choose to project such a pathetic picture of emigrant life? He is perhaps trying to suggest that moving away from self to discover self is a painful process however necessary it may be. This is the grim consolation one of the characters in the novel Tornado comes by: "We got to suffer first and then come together. If there is one thing England going to teach all O' we is that there ain't no place like home no matter how bad home is. But you got to pay to learn, . . ."[7]

In *Of Age and Innocence* Lamming examines the relationship of the returning exile to his native land. The novelist's attitude to this issue of return is ambivalent. Mark Kennedy, a young West Indian intellectual returns home after twenty years since "in all twenty years he was never really at home in England." But back on the island he fails to identify himself with the Caribbean revolution for liberation and afflicted with a sense of failure and guilt he suffers a paralysis of will and flees the island a second time. As Ian Munro points out: "Mark's failure is in part a comment on the continued inability of the colonized West Indian intellectual to return to his roots."[8] In the character of Isaac Shephard, another exile who too returns to join the revolution, Lamming gives us another version of the theme of return. Shephard suffers an acute sense of otherness among the alien people in England and he suddenly discovers how as a colonial he had always lived in the shadow of meaning which others had placed on his presence in the world. He reclaims his ties with his land and instinctively fuses with the history of the people, the more immediate existential conditions of his own emigrant experience. The novelist shows that the human response to a social phenomenon is after all a variable and not constant.

Water with Berries (1971) is Lamming's fullest exploration of the West Indian artist in exile and of the inevitable bankruptcy of the artistic sensibility outside the framework of community. The migration of the West Indian artist to London and how this affects his development both as man and artist is the theme of the novel. The subject here is not West Indian writer per se but three artists – a painter, a musician and an actor – all set in a pathetic pursuit of recognition in an alien society which is totally indifferent to their identity. Lamming uses the tempest myth as the structural framework, subverts the story of European emigration, reverses the journeys and places Caliban in London. The author says:

> Then they (Caliban's descendents) discovered the reality of Prospero's home – not from a distance, not filtered through Prospero's explanations or records of his name, but through their own immediate and dire experience.[9]

In the lives of these three artists, Lamming examines the continuing drama of conflict and rejection that attends West Indian domiciled in Great Britain. All the three make frantic efforts to make their voices heard fighting anonymity and a constant threat of annihilation. They finally resort to acts of violence against the society in which they sought refuge. Their dreams of success in the metropolis are consumed in the flames of despair and revolt and their art dies soundlessly.

Lamming's fictional work thus shows a continuing preoccupation with the related themes of exile, emigration and expatriation and the author's position in relation to these issues has been shifting from time to time. He considers exile as a necessary though painful recourse open to a Caribbean frustrated in a society that is rendered culturally sterile. Then he quickly adds that expatriation is a painful tryst with anonymity. He considers the possibility of return with a sense of nostalgia but realizes that there can be no smooth slipping back into a slot that belongs to one. Return does not appear to be either desirable or possible as yet. It is equally certain that one can never find a home outside one's home.

What emerges from all these reflections of the writer, is a kind of "no win situation." One wonders if there is a way out of this impasse.

Lamming provides no conclusive answers, but views the situation as one in the process of evolution. "The dilemma of the West Indian writer abroad," as Lamming succinctly sums up, is "he hungers for nourishment from a soil which he could not at present endure."[10] They have no option but to wait, wait until such a time comes when their islands emerge more inhabitable from the throes of cultural revolution. Lamming adds that an expatriate writer has a specific role to play in this cultural revolution. He says: "My role it seems has rather to do with time and change than with the geography of circumstance."[11]

The expatriate Caribbean writer waits with hope and expectation for a social and cultural change to take place in his islands, and continues to draw from and contribute to this movement. C.L.R. James, one of the most powerful spokespersons of the West Indian consciousness, expressed the same sentiment almost half a century ago: "It is when you are outside, but can take part as a member, that you see differently from the ways they see, and you are able to write independently."[12] "Take part as a member" – this is what Lamming has been doing for almost four decades. Living abroad, he kept going back to and fro and getting involved in what he calls "extra curricular activity"[13] including tasks as varied as editing Barbados and Guyana Independence issues and lending support to Rastafari movement. All his work, literary and political, centres round a desire for change of values in his society. The new generation of Caribbean writers too hold a broadly similar position. On this issue of expatriation Caryl Philips speaking for his generation of Caribbean expatriate writers says that they continue to have attachment to two places and that their work is spun out of "the tension between two places." He adds:

> And although the price to be paid for continuing to have an attachment to both places is high in terms of emotional financial and material cost and the resultant sense of almost permanent displacement, this price is not as high as that which would be demanded from me were I to beat a romantic retreat to the unmarked, unnamed, much-imagined villa in the sun where inevitably like the river that does not know its own source, the writer's pen begins to dry up.[14]

On a close reading we find that all Caribbean writers from C.L.R. James through Lamming and Walcott to Caryl Philips continue to inhabit two worlds and turn the pain of this dual existence into the revolutionary power of their work. Let us hope with Caryl Philips that living and writing in the Caribbean would soon become a reality for them.

NOTES

1. George Lamming, "The West Indian People" in *Caribbean Essays*, ed. Andrew Salkey (London: Evans Brothers, 1972), p. 5.
2. George Lamming, *In the Castle of My Skin* (London: Michael Joseph, 1953), p. 299.
3. George Lamming, "Interview" by Frank Birbal Singh in *Journal of Commonwealth Literature*, vol. 23, no. 1 (1988), pp. 182-88.
4. Ngugi wa Thiong'o, *Homecoming* (London: Heinemann, 1970), p. 128.
5. George Lamming, *The Emigrants* (1954; London and New York: Allison and Busby, 1980), p. 66.
6. George Lamming, "The West Indian People," p. 10.
7. George Lamming, *The Emigrants*, p. 77.
8. Ian Munro, "George Lamming" in *West Indian Literature*, ed. Bruce King (London: MacMillan, 1979), p. 135.
9. George E. Kent: "A Conversation with George Lamming," *Black World*, 22, no. 5 (March 1973), p. 89.
10. George Lamming, *The Pleasures of Exile* (London: Michael Joseph, 1960), p. 50.
11. *Ibid.*
12. C.L.R. James quoted in Caryl Philip, "Living and Writing in the Caribbean: An Experiment," *Kunapipi*, vol. XI, no. 2 (1989), p. 50.
13. George Lamming, "Interview," p. 186.
14. Caryl Philips, "Living and Writing in the Caribbean," p 49.

An Inscrutability: Forster's Vision of India

MANJUSHREE S. KUMAR

The title, *A Passage to India* closely resembles the title of one of Walt Whitman's poems, and this is how Forster's search for a meaning of the unspelt, the mysteries of mankind, begins. The Indian civilization had come to signify a totality, and the mythico-philosophical reality of India kept the English in awe of the country. The period of imperialism i.e. the British rule in India could be perceived as the Englishman's groping for the Indian reality. The latter existed as a mighty embodiment of a statement of life, a truth which was being illegitimately harnessed and unduly chained. The historical fact of the English domination engaged the English in a corporate act and the perception of themselves to a large extent, was that of a collective identity. But strangely enough, they couldn't venture beyond a certain limit of India's more physical realities and attributes. They could only come up to a point, beyond which India became the unknowable, the mystery – a reality to be understood, a truth to be grasped. Shamsul Islam observes in *Chronicles of the Raj:* "For Kipling too India is a metaphysical being that frustrates all efforts at coming to terms with it which negates all our values and modes of perception." (23) Kipling's *Kim* reflects this idea at its core, and Daphne Manners at the temple in *The Raj Quartet*, reveals her desire to fathom the depths of the Indian reality. The uneasiness of Sarah, Barbie and Lady Manners' conscience (again in *The Raj Quartet*) remains unallayed, as the Indian remains for them the "unknown Indian." The mysterious sound in the Marabar Caves in E.M. Forster's *A Passage to India* is supremely symbolic of what remained hidden and unknown. *A Passage to India* is the product of Forster's two visits to India in 1912-13 and 1921. His second visit to India in 1921 was in the capacity of private secretary to the Maharajah of Dewas Senior, about which he later wrote: "It was the great opportunity of my life," when he could see "so much of the side of life that is hidden from most English people."[1]

Although Cyril Fielding in *A Passage to India* remarks (when he is asked to express his views on political issues): "I cannot tell you why England is here or whether she ought to be here. It's beyond me,"[2] this book is not a political treatise. Forster is concerned with larger, more essential issues. The incident of the Marabar Caves defines and gives *A Passage to India* its philosophical contour. India is an enigma for both Forster and Kipling and is described by the latter as "the great Sphinx of the Plains." That nothing is clear-cut and evades all focus becomes a leitmotif in *A Passage to India*. Fielding explains: "A mystery is only a high-sounding term for a muddle," and continues "Aziz and I know that India's a muddle." (86) This inscrutability is repeatedly suggested in the novel. Adela observes at the polo match, a greenish bird flying into the trees and Ronny is supposed to identify it. This becomes impossible.

As Forster takes us to the Marabar Caves, we are told that the caves are dark and even though they open towards the sun, little or no light penetrates through them. Striking a match here, only heightens their mystery and their reality remains concealed. The caves are "contemporaneous with the beginning of creation, the time of the Genesis."[3]

The mystery which has philosophy as substance envelops and even shows the way to Forster's vision of India. In the cave "there is little to see and no eye to see it." (138) Both the observer and the object elude each other. The caves acquire an enormity that must impinge on the consciousness of man. His position in the universe is immediately a function of how he must relate to these uncanny manifestations of the physical creation. The caves show no direction, no outward meaningful indications: "An entrance was necessary, so mankind made one." (139) The closer Forster approaches the Indian reality, the more esoteric it becomes. The caves emerge from a void and lead to nothing concrete; a nothingness. Forster expresses his notion of the caves' non-existence in: "a bubble-shaped cave that has neither ceiling nor floor, and mirrors its own darkness in every direction infinitely." (139)

Forster records the highly enthusiastic reactions of Adela Quested and Mrs. Moore as they travel to the Marabar Caves. The landscape, as they observe, is endowed with all its physical attributes—the pattern of trees, the throbbing colour and the most magical change of shades and hues. But with all this phenomenal, the passage of night and the dawn of day, the arrival of the "supreme moment," suddenly "nothing occurred." (149) The two points in phenomenal existence—one when something transpires or happens and the other when there is a nothingness of state, emerges more and more convincingly as Forster's perception of the mystery.

There is also a shrouded sense of the kind of relationship that develops between Dr. Aziz, Mrs. Moore, Adela Quested and Fielding. On the occasion of the visit to the Marabar Caves, Aziz asks Mrs. Moore whether she remembered the Mosque where they had met and developed a friendship. He feels overwhelmingly cordial and friendly: "Friendships last longest that begin like that, I think." (155) Answering questions about the greatest of the Moghul emperors, Aziz has something very peremptory to state about India. "Nothing embraces the whole of India, nothing, nothing." (156) And Adela has an answer to: "There will have to be something universal in this country," and the moment something tangible was suggested, (in conformity to the leitmotif) it turned into the vanishing world: "but as soon as it was put into prose it became untrue." (156) Aziz speaks for Forster, as he strikes a note of egalitarianism: "This picnic is nothing to do with English or Indians; it is an expedition of friends." (170)

We return at this point to the visit to the Marabar Caves. The caves were entered through a large, back hole and soon the caves merging with the landscape became a cosmic symbol. "Before man, with his itch for the seemly, had been born, the planet must have looked thus. The Kite flapped away. . . . Before birds, perhaps. . . . And then the hole belched, and humanity returned." (158) The caves came up with a "terrifying echo" and the sound wrapped in itself layers of mystifying perception: "the same monotonous noise replies and quivers up and down the walls until it is absorbed into the roof." (159) "Boum" as the sound, transcends all human perception of speech or alphabet and comes to denote the universal as first perceived by man. The mystery of the Marabar is integral and forms the focus of consciousness, as Forster delineates India. Timelessness had become a component and 'boum' was the great vastness that enveloped even the divine words of Christianity—'Let there be light' and 'It is finished.' The echo and the 'boum' of the Marabar had extended to the farthest limits of Time and Space. Even towards the end of the cave expedition, there is the incident of Adela Quested getting lost. The frenzy this generates in Aziz is another motif of the mystery that edges all forms of human interaction and events.

Moving from Forster's own vision of India, it becomes relevant to refer to what Paul Scott terms as 'A Post-Forsterian View' in his lecture 'After Marabar: Britain and India, A Post-Forsterian View.' Every successive reading of *A Passage to India*, Scott confesses, increased his admiration for the novel. He sees the novel as one "with a powerful prophetic element, as a philosophical novel, not a social novel."[4] However the reason why he records his observation and details of the English in 1943, as 'Post-Forsterian,' is because of the difference between the Turtons and Burtons and Dr. Aziz, and the English and Indians Scott himself met in shops, railway stations, in ante-rooms and messes.

A sense of the inscrutable dawns as much on Scott (in fact more decisively), as on any other discerning reader. He refers to the passage with which *A Passage to India* ends: "But the horses didn't want it—they swerved apart; the earth didn't want it, sending up rocks through which riders must pass single file; the temples, the tank, the jail, the palace, the birds, the carrion, the Guest House, that came into view as they issued from the gap and saw Mau beneath; they didn't want it, they said in their hundred voices, 'No, not yet' and the sky said 'No, not there.'" (316) It is the "No, not there" which puzzles. After all when and where can Aziz and Fielding be friends? The possibilities are numerous and "Its subtleties are endless."[5] The Marabar Caves once again figure as "a particular civilization's terminus," a symbol against which a duality will metamorphose, and there would result—an amalgamation. There is the philosophical parallel of Mrs. Moore "sitting motionless with horror" and T.S. Eliot's "still as we may sit we must be still moving." Scott draws on Mrs. Moore's experience of the Marabar Caves and connects it with a contemporary context. Her feeling of the void is echoed in the fear of the western civilization "that indeed everything exists and nothing has value." This points to the element of prophecy in the novel.

Literary criticism places *A Passage to India* on the plane of the acting out of the liberal dilemma. Forster had made it amply clear through his own vision that the liberal idea could work and that it was coming into the ascendancy. What remained undecided, even arbitrary, was the confrontation in India as one between Indian nationalism and an alien rule. However, Fieldingism both in Britain and India referred to a common cause: "a belief in the essentially dynamic nature of man" and a promise of "individual freedom, social justice and equal opportunities." In Forster's British India, the Anglo-Indian connection was sustained largely through acquiescence on the part of the ruled. Fieldingism, as does the thrust of certain characters as Sarah Layton, Daphne Manners and Barbie Batchelor in *The Raj Quartet*, lived and asserted itself, but only to discover that it generated greater confrontation. In the post-Forsterian British India, Scott notes, the English were "no longer completely in tune with the changing national ethos."[6] Forster's Turtons and Burtons had basked in the Edwardian sunlight, but they were to become more and more alienated with the disturbing decline of imperialism. An existence of illusion was marked for them.

Although the post-Forsterian view points to some differences, there is enough, in the Anglo-Indian connection of 1913, that lies close to Scott's perception (1943) of the closeness of the two races. Scott speaks of the context of work in which he casts his Indian characters, and that through this, they come close to "what connects us than to what divides us, as human beings."[7] Forster's Aziz and Mrs. Moore discover the closeness between them, when through a fortuity, they meet at the mosque. The description of the front of the mosque as Aziz stood gazing in the moonlight brings out a wholeness and totality that was inherent in the heart of the Indian: "The contrast between this dualism and the contention of shadows within pleased Aziz, and he tried to symbolize the whole into some truth of religion or love." (41)

India's philosophy and religion get depicted through the Cosmic play of Lord Krishna: "And the Lord bounds hither and thither through the aisles, chance, and the sport of chance, irradiating little mortals with His immortality." (286-87) Forster had felt the pulse of the inscrutable in India, but the essence of the soul of India was evidently beyond the reach of the English, and India was to be grasped as a might of a truth. For Forster India's consciousness was one that reached the farthest territories of the profundity of universe, and knew all "to its uttermost depth." (149)

NOTES

1. E.M. Forster, *The Hill of Devi* (London, 1953), p. 10.

2. E.M. Forster, *A Passage to India* (1924; Harmondsworth, Middlesex: Penguin, 1986), p. 124.
3. Shamsul Islam, *Chronicles of the Raj* (London: Macmillan, 1979), p. 20.
4. Shelley C. Reece, ed. *My Appointment with the Muse: Essays, 1961-75* (London: Heinemann, 1986), p. 123.
5. *Ibid.*, p. 124.
6. *Ibid.*, p. 126.
7. *Ibid.*, p. 127.

In Search of Order: A Study of V.S. Naipaul and Attia Hosain

NOVY KAPADIA

In the quest for identity, in the search for order in rapidly changing societies, there are certain remarkable similarities in Attia Hosain's *Sunlight on a Broken Column* and V.S. Naipaul's *A House for Mr. Biswas*. Both the novels were published in 1961. The protagonists of both novels are alienated individuals seeking solace in a world of cultural confusion. Both novels aptly chronicle the stages in the loss of old value systems and customs. *In Sunlight on a Broken Column*, the narrator heroine Laila reveals how the throes of partition, destroys the fabric of the feudal world, the hierarchy and rigid codes of her talukdar family, compelling people to make a choice. In *A House for Mr. Biswas*, we also witness the gradual disintegration of the Hindu joint family system and the world of rituals, customs and caste.

In Naipaul's novels, we witness the expatriate experience, a minority culture adapting to a cosmopolitan society, the changing value systems and its impact on the characters of the novel. Naipaul cleverly shows the change in the novel from a pre-occupation with fate and caste to a pre-occupation with money and ambition in the later stages of the novel. Mohun Biswas is married to Shama, as he is of the right (Brahmin) caste. It is a marriage of convenience, in which the fact that Biswas has a meagre source of income as a sign painter is irrelevant. Barely a decade later, there is also a marriage of convenience but with a difference. The search for a wife for the elder son of the Tulsi family (or the 'elder God' as mimicked by Mohun Biswas) shows the growing consumerism and changing value systems. The chancy haste of the earlier marriages, based solely on caste were ignored. There were other concerns for the choice of the bride. The most suitable bride was to be found only amongst families in soft drinks, or with cinemas and filling stations. Money rather than caste or religion were the motivating factors in deciding a marriage partner for Shekhar: "And at last, in a laxly Presbyterian family with one filling station, two lorries, a cinema and some land, they found a girl."[1] (230)

In contrast, Attia Hosain's novel presents the minority (Muslim) perspective of the traumas and upheavals of partition. The author has told the story of the big talukdar household from the intimacy of felt experience and yet from the distant point of recollection (1961). The main character Laila, her cousins Asad and Saleem, like the Indians of Trinidad in Naipaul's novels, are alienated, in a rapidly changing world. They are in quest of a new identity, a new social role amidst the tensions and violence of the times. The novel chronicles the stages in Laila's life from adolescence to maturity in the midst of political upheavals. Similarly Mohun Biswas and his family shift from country to town, from Hindi to English and from a sprawling joint family system to a nuclear family and independence for one's family. Hence both novels are dealing not just with the history of Mr. Mohun Biswas or Laila but the movement of cultures. The search for order, identity amidst social change is what both Attia Hosain and V.S. Naipaul set out to explore.

Both Mohun Biswas and Laila have deprived childhoods. Laila, an orphan, is brought up in the household of her grandfather Baba Jan. Mohun Biswas is branded unlucky as a child and told to stay away from water. Ironically it is his father who dies through drowning though Biswas is indirectly responsible for it. So as a teenager, Mohun Biswas has a lonely existence. The social role expected of both Mohun Biswas and Laila are chalked out by the demands and pressures of their family systems. In the orthodox world of ritual, prayers and customs and the Hindu joint family, Biswas is ordained to be trained as a priest. It is not due to any pious inclinations but because he is a Brahmin, the right caste. He is sent to Pandit Jairam to learn Hindi, some important scriptures and various ceremonies. His apprenticeship is brief. He defiles Jairam's oleander tree which fulfils the prediction of his horoscope that much harm will be averted if he is kept away from trees and water. So ironically his horoscope and being branded unlucky is a catalyst which drives him away from the Indian world. He becomes the lonely expatriate seeking a new social role. The Indian world is shrinking and Biswas has to seek identity in a world of cross-cultural connections. The world of the talukdars in which Laila is born works on a principle of strict role-restriction based on gender by clearly marking off male and female domains. "Read the Holy Book, remeber Allah and his Prophet, then women will fight to choose you for their sons."[2] (14) This is the advice of an ageing, occasionally overbearing but loving nurse Hakiman Bua. Laila's expected social role is to be a model wife. Like Mohun Biswas she refuses to conform.

She asserts her opposition to this stereotype, docile role by her hobby of voracious reading. Education for women is permitted but not excessive reading, as it could lead to a questioning mind. Hakiman Bua represents traditional opinion and family beliefs when she chides Laila for excessive scholarship and constant reading in Baba Jan's library. The assumption is that the proper place for the women is the zenana or the female quarters. Trespassing into male territory, physical or figurative is frowned upon. So the process of segregation, of straitjacketing into a narrowly-defined female identity begins right in early childhood.

Laila, the orphaned child rebels against such straitjacketing. She starts with the initial advantage of being spared the rigorous discipline deemed fit for a traditional Muslim, the kind of upbringing her cousin Zahra is subjected to. Laila's doubts and misgivings about what traditional codes demand of her serve as a comment on conventional mores and values. Her idiosyncrasies, playing with Nandi the servant girl, defying elders and her loneliness which bred in her a love for reading, were not considered seemly in a growing girl. Hence Hakiman Bua's plaintive cry:

> Your books will eat you. They will dim the light of your lovely eyes, my moon Princess, and then who will marry you, owl-eyed, peering through glasses. (14)

Laila's struggle and quest for emancipation, reveals the winds of change in feudal and aristocratic Muslim homes, ushered in by British liberal education. The novel however shows that a shake-up in the feudal shake-up dictated by political exigencies did not fully "challenge male dominance within the family or community." Laila's stepping out of her cliched role and struggle for individual freedom is a personal effort.

Similarly Mohun Biswas is a rebel by temperament and refuses to conform to the demands of an orthodox society. Biswas felt trapped when married to Shama, he fell into the clutches of Tulsidom at Hanuman House. Naipaul depicts Hanuman House as a symbol of traditionalism, ritual duty, hierarchy and rigidity. Fixed roles for the inmates of the house led to an awareness of duties, conventions and rituals. Biswas refuses to submit, to submerge his individual identity to this apparent monolith of conventions and prejudices. Thus he refuses to feel inferior to the Tulsis, though he has no money to his credit. Instead he actually feels better than they are because he has strong intellectual interests, ambitions for greatness and an independent mind. He differentiates himself by speaking Creole English in Hanuman House while everyone else speaks Hindi. He ridicules 'constipated Hari' the symbol of religious reverence and ceremony. His initial revolt is often instinctive and somewhat futile. With his skill at mimicry and verbal inventions he rebels against an imposed order. Mrs. Tulsi is nicknamed the 'old hen' and her sons Owad and Shekher are called 'Little Gods.' His wit and rebelliousness enables him to maintain his identity in the cloistered environment of the Tulsi household. He quickly spots the contradiction in the behaviour of the 'Little Gods' who attend Hindu pujas wearing crucifixes. Similarly a sister-in-law Chinta recites Hindu incantations in combination with a candle and crucifix. Biswas' reactions to such practices are like a blow to the moral fabric and halo of the Tulsis who fancy themselves as the last bastion of Hinduism. It is similar to the instance where Laila defends a wronged servant girl against a libertine relative's accusations and is severely reprimanded by her guardian for her audacity. Her act reveals a great deal about the dynamics of oriental paternalistic systems. Similarly Biswas with his individuality and independent mind reveals the hypocrisy and illogicality which creep into a tradition-bound and closed society.

As the novel progresses, Naipaul repeatedly shows the occasionally subtle and sometimes obvious way in which the Western-oriented Creole culture of Trinidad corrodes Hindu traditional customs and beliefs. He also cleverly delineates the shifting of attitudes and psychological bewliderment that this process produces. So it is the combination of the external forces of Westernization and urbanization aided by the internal human impulses which leads to the decay of the highly structured social organization of Hanuman House. The movement away from Arwacas to Port of Spain is an indicator of the gradual disintegration of the joint family system and the inadequacy of the ancestral home in the face of modern aspirations. The role of education is also vital in the decay of the traditional Hindu society. For instance it is Biswas' education which makes him think differently from theirs. It is for the interests of Owad's education that Mrs. Tulsi leaves her home at Arwacas and goes into five-day-a-week residence in Port-of-Spain, because of its well-equipped schools. So in the novel, formal education has a disintegrating influence. Naipaul also shows that for the second generation of Indian children like Owad, Anand and Savi, education is a chance for rapid upward social mobility and a new identity in society. The importance to education in this novel, has a strong historical and autobiographical element. Earlier in Trinidad one third of the educational budget was spent on secondary education for a handful of boys whose parents were wealthy. Monied groups were mostly white and fair-skinned so that the question of colour and discriminationn was often voiced as regards admission to secondary schools.[3] The exhibition that Anand and Savi competed for was the authorities' attempt to democratize education in Trinidad. Naipaul satirizes the middle-class aspirations and proportion of martyrdom the parents underwent to ensure that their children entered secondary schools with a scholarship or 'exhibition' as it was called. Anand is placed on a special brain-food diet of milk and prunes and undergoes intense preparation:

> He went from school to the Dairies to school again; . . . Leaving home at seven in the morning, he returned at half past six. He ate. Then he did his school home-work; then he prepared for all his private lessons. (463)

Examination day is like a sacrificial day. Naipaul parodies such middle-class aspirations and pretensions. However besides the humour the underlying message is that even for traditional Hindu families, success in education is now of paramount importance. The rigorously drilled pupils are in search of scholarships to pursue higher education, which can get them lucrative jobs as professionals, either lawyers or doctors, and improve the status of their family. C.L.R. James, the distinguished historian, political theorist and commentator, says that this materialistic approach to education in Trinidad and other islands of the West Indies in the mid-twentieth century led to the emergence of a black middle class often alienated from the people.[4] The importance given to education and the attentiveness to small details enables the author chronicle the history of a culture, changes in value systems and the search for a new order.

In *Sunlight on a Broken Column*, there is also the movement of the times. British liberal education has led to a questioning of the rigid hierarchy and values of the talukdar family. After the death of grandfather Baba Jan, the controlling power in the family is Uncle Hamid with his liberal western education. Moving with the times means learning English, "which is what the young men want now." The reform-minded Hamid wants the girls to have the education, "that will best fit them for their responsibilities in this changing world." This liberal outlook and impact of the freedom struggle has an impact on the sensitive Laila. She makes a plea for personal freedom in a society which works with a communal identity and clearly-defined sex roles. Her love affair with Ameer Hussain, a junior lecturer at Aligarh Muslim University and lower in status than her talukdar family gives her meaning in life. The author shows that the doubts and queries that occur in her are the results of her exposure to liberal education and western notions of equality, liberty and individualism. So she cannot relate to the confined world of family alliances and myriad taboos. By her marriage to Ameer, Laila forsakes the security of her comfortable house and the values of an Islamic talukdar family for an uncertain emancipation. Her act is a symbolic gesture challenging the paternalistic structures.

In Naipaul's novel, the vision of a house of his own, for Mr. Biswas adds a new dimension to his experience. The house stands for status, security, order and beauty. In his early novels, the house is a very dominant image. In *Miguel Street* (1959) the house is simply a spot from which the street can be viewed, an excuse for being there. In *The Mystic Masseur* (1957), Ganesh's new house in Fuente Grove, is the image of a compromise. In *The Mimic Men* (1967) there are a series of houses which are the temporary residences of ship-wrecked people, all expressions of expatriate taste. However in *A House for Mr. Biswas* (1961) the house is a central unifying symbol. The yearning for a house is not just a middle-class dream for Mr. Biswas but a statement that he is more than just a rebellious buffoon and a person capable of leaving on the world the marks of his existence. The house becomes his identity. When Mr. Biswas eventually moves into his heavily mortgaged house in Sikkim Street, it is not just an act of middle-class security and identity. The result of the movement is that Mr. Biswas's claims on his children and his wife Shama are finally consummated. They arrive in Sikkim Street a united family. The movement to house in Sikkim Street is also a point of resolution in Naipaul's early work, as regards expatriate experience. The author suggests that when all the ironies and contradictions have had their say it is better to accept some of the values of the West and declare independence for oneself and one's family. Similarly in *Sunlight on a Broken Column*, the image of the house acquires different meanings. Part IV of the novel shows that in material terms, her rebellion was a failure. The house she stayed in with Ameer was barely bigger than her room in her ancestral world. There were no scores of servants as in Hasanpur and Ashiana. Yet when the narrator-heroine Laila after partition walks through the rooms of Ashiana, there is the human impulse of nostalgia but she does not wish for the old order to return. Her ancestral home is associated with the cloistered feudal order. Her new-found identity and struggle to be Ameer's lover and then wife, curbs any desire for a return to the paternalistic, hierarchical structure of the past.

Both the novelists wrote in the 1960s, the decade of counter-culture, rebellion and flower power, of barricades and the Vietnam War, Beatles and Rolling Stones. They wrote about an age of social turbulence, the 1930s-1940s, as colonies sought independence from the shackles of colonial rule. These factors gave the non-conformity of their characters an identity and a certitude. Non-conformity was thus the badge of authenticity, for the protagonists of both the novels.

NOTES

1. V.S. Naipaul, *A House for Mr. Biswas* (Harmondsworth, Middlesex, England: Penguin, 1969).
2. Attia Hosain, *Sunlight on a Broken Column* (Delhi: Arnold Heinemann, 1979).
3. Katrak Ketu, "Decolonizing Culture: Toward a Theory for Postcolonial Women's Texts," *Modern Fiction Studies*, Spring 1989, vol. 35, no. 1, p. 168.
4. Kenneth Ramchand, *The West Indian Novel and Its Background* (London: Faber and Faber, 1978).
5. C.L.R. James, *Beyond a Boundary* (London: Hutchinson, 1963).
6. Landeg White, *V.S. Naipaul: A Critical Introduction* (London: 1975), p. 153.

V.S. Naipaul: An Expatriate

VASANT PATEL

V.S. Naipaul seems to have a very complex personality. He is an Indian Brahmin uprooted from the land of his ancestors. It is a known fact that his grandfather migrated to Trinidad as an indentured labourer. Secondly, he is West Indian by his birth and growth. Finally, he lives as an expatriate in London because of his self-made exile. Obviously, these three factors are largely responsible for the shaping of his personality. Indeed, they are important in the making up of his mind.

Naipaul's 'magnificent obsession is India' as he himself admits.[1] But his way of thinking as seen in his books is British though he is West Indian by birth and growth. His position, his viewpoint is not infalliable because of this strange sensibility which can be appropriately termed as 'expatriate sensibility' as well.

There has been a lot of misunderstanding by critics – Indian and Western – about Naipaul's book on India: *An Area of Darkness, An Overcrowded Barracoon* and *India*: *A Wounded Civilization*. The assessment of Naipaul on India brings several other points into focus. The basic point is the problem of sensibility. It is the sensibility of a person that affects his judgements and viewpoints. To make an authentic and objective assessment of a phenomenon, two points are to be kept in mind. 'Who' judges and 'Who' or 'What' is judged. The judgement may not always be free from limitations. Here, the problem of sensibility is involved. Hence, the classification of Naipaul's sensibility is important. It is 'the starting point of this inquiry'[2] as Naipaul states in his preface to *A Wounded Civilization*.

Naipaul's approach to Indian life and culture can be understood only in terms of his expatriate sensibility and his triple identity. He assesses Indian life and culture with the Hindu norms of karma, dharma and moksha and the Western norms of individuality and freedom. The Indian self accepts things with faith whereas the

Western self challenges or examines from the individual point of view. Naipaul's feeling is not contempt but pain at the plight and predicament of India. Naipaul's assessment is of an un-believer Hindu totally ignorant of Hinduism. He himself is not responsible for being an unbeliever, an ignorant Hindu but his ancestors and family background are responsible.

The Hindu theory of karma propounds faith. Hinduism is a religion of faith in god. It preaches faith in religious rituals and principles. There is no room for individual freedom or reason. Faith and devotion are basic virtues. This element of faith sometimes assumes blindness and it is at times challenged or shaken with logic. Hindus accept religious matters without any doubt or challenge. They patiently accept what they get as a result of karma. Religious preachings are accepted as Dharma against which nothing is said or done. The righteousness of action never matters, the mandate of the preacher matters. Devotees accept preachings with reverence and regard without bothering for logic or legitimacy.

Dom Moraes accepts Naipaul as "a writer of our times."[3] Moraes views *An Area of Darkness* in a larger perspective and he feels sorry that it "has come in for much unwarranted criticism in India." He calls it "not only a brilliant piece of literature but an interesting psychological study of Naipaul by Naipaul." This approval of Moraes speaks voluminously. It hints at the fact that *An Area of Darkness* reveals Naipaul and not India. The opinion of Naipaul is based on impression rather than information. It is a picture of India as Naipaul sees it.

Let us first take up statements showing Naipaul's conscious probing into his Brahminism and his deep-rooted Brahmin upbringing contributing to the belief that Naipaul is essentially on the side of India, rather than against it. Naipaul states:

> I came of a family that abounded with pundits. But I had been born an unbeliever. I took no pleasure in religious ceremonies. They were too long and the food came only at the end. I did not understand the language – it was as if our elders expected our understanding would be instincitve – and no one explained the prayers or the ritual . . . my uncle often put it to me that my denial was an admissible type of Hinduism. Examining myself I found only that sense of the difference of people, which I have tried to explain, a vague sense of caste, and a horror of the un-

clean.[4]

Thus Naipaul himself appears to be feeling that his Hindu upbringing has left in him "a vague sense of caste, and a horror of the unclean" as he has mentioned in his Autobiography in which we find the depth of Naipaul's Hindu self. Naipaul emphasizes the Brahmin standpoint from which the stories were written by his father and claims it as also his standpoint. Naipaul himself also was annoyed at the intact continuation of the Hindu base of childhood and youth, in the diversified culture of Trinidad. He himself marvels at the deep-rooted Hinduism in him. Besides the marvel of upbringing there was also a deep impression, which shows that there is a pervasive sense of older Hindu traditional brahmin side of him. Its proof is the reference to Katha arranged in Trinidad. The Hindu growth of Naipaul is so prevalent in him that he is outraged to hear that in Bombay people used candles and electric bulbs for the Diwali festivals and not the rustic claylamps which his family still used in Trinidad.

His first meeting with Ramachandra Dube is full of joy but the second visit is full of dismay and revulsion at the poverty, evident in Ramachandra's person. His early joy melts away. He appears rude, anxious to leave. Naipaul seeks escape when Ramachandra asks for help telling that his grandfather's land is reduced to only 90 acres. The graph of his emotions leading to 'flight' cannot cope with guilt of poverty being responsible for the fate of Ramachandra and the village which is his own too by blood. Naipaul has said of Ramachandra that he could scarcely look at his emaciated body.

Naipaul's insight into India by and large shows him to be far above the judgement of the traveller. He has a privilege of Indian ancestry. Enright[5] is right when he says that Naipaul has the sensibility of a Brahmin but not the supporting beliefs or complacence or callousness. Naipaul's writing on India reveals that a root Brahmin sensibility has been overlaid with a western vision as a result of which ultimately there is no home for him in India: "His assumptions are too much of the West."[6] Walsh too has pointed to the friction of the two sides of his nature which introduce not warmth but despair. This friction seems to contribute to Naipaul's criticism of India.

Strangely enough, within a very short time, Naipaul experiences the security and joy of belonging to country and having a home, when his Brahmin sensibility relates his experience in India to what he had experienced as a boy in Trinidad. At such moments Naipaul wishes to remain open to the "presence" of the country. But, having failed to get experience and familiar awareness of children Naipaul tends to attack India with a Western bias, on the basis of Western categories and makes generalized illogical statements. When he makes a high handed critique of the Indian 'underdeveloped' personality type, his is the Western point of view:

> India's intellectual second-ratedness which is generally taken for granted but may be the most startling and depressing fact about the world's second most populous country, which now has little to offer the world except its Gandhian concept of holy poverty and the recurring crooked comedy of its holy men.[7]

Naipaul's split sensibility contributes to this harsh remark. He is guided by his Western outlook and it appears as if he is a spokesman of England in particular and the Western world in general. He forgets the fact that India has offered a lot to the world.

Naipaul is alternatively both, an Indian in India and a Westerner in India and this dual position causes all problems. Naipaul's joy, exhilaration, exaltation, scintillation come from his Brahmin self, his anger and negativity from the inherent Western self. Naipaul's attitude of sympathy and compassion for Muslims is also because of his guilt at the contempt in which they are held by Hindus—by their being classified as "unclean." Naipaul is not critical of Muslims for their dirt as he is critical of dirt and defecation in India. Naipaul talks too much of defecation: "Indians defecate everywhere." C.D. Narasimhaiah defends:

> A little imaginative sympathy could have helped to soften his irritation at it. After all it is a relic of a predominantly agricultural society in the process of transforming itself into the urban but not having resources equal to the ever increasing emigration. Of landless labourers—they are literally flooding the city sights which are aesthetically far more revolting than defecation.[8]

V.S. Naipaul writes for English-speaking people. He never cared for the land of his own birth and his people. He admits it was a mistake to have been born there, that he always wished to forget it. Trinidad was for him a "destitute society," without history, without achievement, it is unlikely, he cared for India. When he cannot show a gratitude to his birthplace, how can one expect a gratitude to India, his ancestors's birthplace?

Apparently, Naipaul is in search of an identity. Originally a Hindu Brahmin self, disinterested in rituals, tries to find in India what he expected but unfortunately with the fusion of British self does not find solace. He remains totally homeless without any brand of identity. Only a split sensibility. Homelessness[9] is the only word fit to describe his condition, Naipaul should concede that the Indian community in Trinidad was more homogeneous to him.

Naipaul discussess the case of Ramnath the steno and Hiralal the typist to prove that Indians feel it a degradation to carry out the work which is not expected of them. But Naipaul seems to forget the fact that this type of awareness is a gift to Indians from British people. As such Indians never feel humiliation in doing any work. Gandhi is an example of a man who advocated that every work is humble and no work is mean. Hundreds of people undertake to manual work in America. Indians never consider labour a degradation. Naipaul's observation that Indians prefer the lower bunk while travelling in Railway is also not infalliable as it is actually a matter of choice, and many men prefer the upper bunk only. So, it appears that the criticism regarding Ramnath is owing to his British self. In South Africa a white British felt humiliated in sitting with black Gandhi. When mere sitting is a humiliation why not typing which is obviously the typist's job.

Naipaul's sensibility seems to be caste sensibility at times. There is only one Hindu group in India that escapes caricature or criticism. It is evidently the Brahmin family he travels with from Avantipur to Srinagar. Naipaul experiences the feeling of being at home in India for the first time.

C.D. Narasimhaiah says that as a darkman in white society disowning him Naipaul—he will never be considered an Englishman—should be offended by passing uncomplimentary reference to England because he has chosen to live there in pursuit of success. Naipaul is a success seeker and a stranger to the centre of wholeness, and having gone to England at the age of 18 on a Government scholarship had not even cared to look back at the parents—so obsessed he was with success he would not respond to his dying father's last wish to see his son.

The contempt of Naipaul for India is owing to his British self. He describes Trinidad society as disintegrating. As intellectual and "conscience keeper of society" he cannot escape his own share in hastening its disintegration. However, Naipaul seems to be changed in his approach and outlook, the latest book *India: A Million Mutinies Now* seems to show Naipaul more compassionate.

NOTES

1. Andrew Robinson, "The Weekly cover story" (An Interview with V.S. Naipaul), *The Illustrated Weekly of India*, July 5-11, 1987.
2. V.S. Naipaul, *India: A Wounded Civilization*, p. 9.
3. Dom Moraes, "A Writer for our Times," *Gentleman*, February 1984, pp. 36-39.
4. V.S. Naipaul, *An Area of Darkness*, p. 32.
5. D.J. Enright, "Who is India," *Encounter*, December 1964, pp. 59-64.
6. Landeg White, *V.S. Naipaul*, p. 7.
7. *India: A Wounded Civilization*, p. 104.
8. C.D. Narasimhaiah, "V.S. Naipaul: A Case of Bizarre Reputation," in *The Function of Criticism in India*, ed. C.D. Narasimhaiah (Mysore: Central Institute of Indian Languages, 1986), pp. 117-51.
9. Paul Therox, *V.S. Naipaul: An Introduction to his Work*, p. 92.

Expatriate Experience in Indian English Poetry

VANDANA DATTA

Alienation is something that every poet suffers from. To be a poet is to be alienated. In the case of Indian English poets, the situation is all the more complicated. The use of a foreign language alienates them further from the general masses. While a Dinkar or a Bachchan can become a highly popular figure, while Rabindranath Tagore can become a household name in Bengal, an Indian English poet just cannot have such aspirations. He is a poet of the elite, at least in India, that is the present situation. It is only abroad that he gets a large audience, hence greater opportunities. This is probably the reason why a number of Indian English poets have either settled, or spent a considerable time, abroad. A.K. Ramanujan was a Professor of Dravidian Linguistics in the USA. B. Rajan, one of the first modern Indian poets, was before his retirement, a Professor of English in Canada. R. Parthasarathy, an editor, has settled down in New York. Dom Moraes has returned to India only a few years ago after having spent a long time abroad. Until recently, Vikram Seth was an editor with the Stanford University Press. Among others, Nissim Ezekiel and Shiv K. Kumar have travelled abroad considerably enough to get a feel of the different cultures of the world. Their works therefore reflect the circumstances and predicaments peculiar to them. It follows then that there is a fairly large bulk of expatriate poetry by Indian English poets.

II

Of all the poets it is probably Ramanujan who has made the best of his expatriate experience. He is what one would call a poet in exile. Parthasarathy's words apply literally to him:

> There is something to be said for exile:
> You learn roots are deep.[1]

Indeed, Ramanujan's long sojourn abroad has inculcated in him a deep awareness of his Indian, rather Hindu, origin. So deep is this obsession with his Indian past that he opens his love poem for his wife on a note of regret:

> Really what keeps us apart
> at the end of years is unshared
> childhood.[2]

No wonder, a large bulk of Ramanujan's poetical works deals with his Indian past. Memories of childhood cover the whole range of his imagination. In a number of poems there is an accurate representation of certain instances. In the poem titled "Snakes" (*SP*, 2-3) Ramanujan, the man, while

> . . . walking in museums of quartz
> or the aisles of bookstacks,

or while,

> touching a book that has gold
> on its spine

thinks of snakes and is reminded of his sister's braids:

> . . . the weave of her knee-long braid has scales,
> their gleaming held by a score of pins.

And all this fear of snakes is traced back to an incident when "a basketful of ritual cobras" had come to his house:

> their brown-wheat glisten ringed with ripples.
> They lick the room with their bodies, curves
> uncurling, writing a sibilant alphabet of panic
> on my floor.

Similarly an early memory of a dead half-naked woman on the beach in the poem "Breaded Fish"

> dry, rolled by the ebb, breaded
> by the grained indifference of sand. (*SP*, 4)

is suddenly revived when the wife prepares breaded fish for him.

Recollection of memory takes a different form in "Of Mothers, among other things." (*SP*, 22) Here the past has been drawn as a contrast to the present. The childhood memories of a glorious past –

> . . . the silk and white
> petal of my mother's youth

– are brought forward when confronted by the bleak, drab present:

> . . . her hands are a wet eagle's
> two black pink-crinkled feet,
>
> one talon crippled in a garden-
> trap set for a mouse. Her sarees
> do not cling: they hang, loose
> feather of a onetime wing.

A more complex strategy has been employed in "History." (*SP*, 47-48) A childhood observation acquires meaning through adult understanding. The scene recalled here is that of the speaker's "little dark aunt" in her dying mother's room looking for something. At that moment the child had thought that she must have been searching "a rolling pin/her little son had brought for play." It is only later when his mother discloses what she had really been looking for:

> her two
> daughters, one dark one fair,
> unknown each to the other
> alternately picked their mother's body clean
> before it was cold
> or the eyes were shut,
>
> of diamond ear-rings,
> bangles, anklets, the pin

> in her hair,
> the toe-rings from her wedding
> the previous century . . .

that he comprehends the whole thing, and his aunt's dark stone face acquires some expression at last. Time present here gains in experience through time past thereby leading to a maturer understanding in time future.

To R. Parthasarathy, the works of Ramanujan are "a signal achievement."[3] To M.K. Naik, however, the achievement is not as great as it could have been possibly because of a "disinclination . . . to have a bold, all-out confrontation with experience, opting instead for sporadic skirmishes, minor engagements and hit and run tactics."[4] He finds in Ramanujan's poems nothing of the complex human situation as developed in William Faulkner's *The Sound and the Fury*. The novel begins with a small girl watching through a window the preparations for the funeral of her grandmother – a picture very similar to that drawn in Ramanujan's poem "History." Out of that picture Faulkner created a masterpiece, while Ramanujan, adds M.K. Naik, "remains content with a casual stroke of minor irony." Such a comparison, however, is not really fair to Ramanujan. One does realize that within the limits of verbal structure in a poem he has succeeded fairly well. Perhaps Faulkner – great as he is – got a much fuller chance in the roomy-canvas of novel-length, and also every other aspect of the novel may have come to his aid. It, therefore, does not seem proper to put Ramanujan to such an obvious disadvantage. If one writes a lyric, it is sufficient if it excels as one. It certainly need not compare with an epic. And if this be the criterion, Ramanujan has to his credit a number of good poems. He has made good of his expatriate experience, the central preoccupation of his works.

It should be noted, however, that nostalgia, as is generally considered, is not the only aspect that colours Ramanujan's poems dealing with his Indian past. What raises these poems above the level of mere social documentation of the Hindu joint family is Ramanujan's poetic sensibility – particularly the way he recapitulates the scene which his memory is able to evoke, and the manner in which he transmutes his experiences into a genuine work of art. There is on the one hand an assured identity with the subject, and on the other a superb detachment. That is to say, the themes so patently subjective, have received an objective treatment. The insider seems to recapitulate the scenes from the distance of an outsider, a distance allowed to him probably by his long sojourn abroad. This recalls to one's mind Eliot's thesis that the man who creates ought to be detached from the man who suffers.[5] And so sharp is the balance between these two selves in Ramanujan that he can even adopt an ironic tone while dealing with his Indian past. In "Obituary," (*SP*, 49) he recalls his father's death and uses the occasion to comment ironically on the rituals associated with the dead·

> Being the burning type
> he burned properly
> at the cremation

For all his avowed declaration of loyalty to Hindu culture, at times Ramanujan assumes a markedly critical stance. In "Conventions of Despair," he writes:

> I must seek and will find
> my particular hell in my hindu mind. (*SP*, 12)

In "A River," (*SP*, 14-15) he criticizes a particular aspect of Hinduism – loss of individuality in the sweep of tradition. In "Small Scale Reflections on a Great House," (*SP*, 40-43) Ramanujan appears to be highly appreciative of the stability and assimilative nature of Hinduism:

> Sometimes I think that nothing
> that ever comes into this house
> goes out. Things come in every day
>
> to lose themselves among other things
> lost long ago among
> other things lost long ago.

One does notice, however, that this is not pure appreciation; there is plenty of wit and irony in the poem. The way he piles up instances reveals the possibility of assimilation itself having a tradition of its own. Both animate and inanimate objects that once enter this house stay on there – "lame wandering cows," "unread library books," "neighbour's dishes," "servants," "phonographs," "epilepsies in the blood," "sons-in-law," "women who come as wives." There is a good deal of irony and taunt in the jumbling together of a wide range of items from sons-in-law to neighbour's dishes and epilepsies.

The vantage point, then, from which Ramanujan writes, rather, most of the Indian expatriate poets write, falls somewhere between the two cultures – Indian and Western. As Bruce King rightly puts it:

> Ramanujan is neither a nostalgic traditionalist nor an advocate of modernization and westernization. He is a product of both and his poems reflect a personality conscious of change, enjoying its vitality, freedom and contradictions, but also aware of memories which form his inner self, memories of an unconscious "namelessness," which are still alive, at the foundations of the self.[14]

Ramanujan's American experiences occur less frequently in his poetry. And where they do, they are generally something apart from his Indian past. The two – his Indian past and the American present – do not intermingle. There is one poem – a wonderful poem too, – however, in which the two cultures clash. In "Still Another View of Grace," (*SP*, 20) a moment of personal crisis is explored: it is a dramatic situation when a girl gives him an inviting look, but he, owing to his Indian upbringing tries to resist the temptation. A conflict of attitudes has been presented which is resolved through an involuntary submission to passion:

> I burned and burned. But one day I turned
> and caught that thought
> by the screams of her hair and said: "Beware.
> Do not follow a gentleman's morals
>
> with that absurd determined air. . . .
> Bred Brahmin among singers of shivering hymns
> I shudder to the bone at hungers that roam the street
> beyond the constable's beat.

The poem is an enactment of an encounter of two cultures, one ancient and the other modern. But the encounter is not merely at the thematic level. The technical genius that Ramanujan is, he presents an encounter at the linguistic level too, evident in the juxtapositions of "priest" and "beast," and in phrases like "shivering hymns" and "screams of hair." The concentrated force in these phrases help in immediately visualizing the scene – a man holding a girl by her hair; the man, a Brahmin brought up amidst strict moral notions, trying to vindicate his morality, ultimately surrendering to passion:

> Commandments crumbled
> in my father's past. Her tumbled hair suddenly known
> as silk in my angry hand, I shook a little
> and took her, behind the laws of my land.

Internal rhymes in this concluding stanza serve to quicken the pace with which the submission occurs. There is something like a sound-pattern in the poem, a pattern built with a purpose so that there is a curious intermingling of language and content. There is a natural musicality in the choice of words, which besides indicating the compulsive nature of the experience also captures the lyricism of the moment.

III

A great admirer of Ramanujan, Parthasarathy seems to be deeply influenced by him in many ways. Acutely conscious of his national heritage, he too explores the various nuances of expatriation. Though widely published in magazines he has only two volumes to his name: *The First Step: Poems* and *Rough Passage*. Done in three sections – "Exile," "Trial" and "Homecoming," the latter like Aurobindo's *Savitri* appears to be a work that will remain in progress throughout the poet's life by continuous editings, revisions and additions.

To come to the first section "Exile," as the name suggests, is about alienation. Not to mention the racial prejudices the Indians have to suffer, there is even more disillusionment to come. The real London is most unlike the London of imagination:

> the city is no jewel, either:
>
> lanes full of smoke and litter,
> with puddles of unwashed
> English children. (*RP*, 15)

This is too much to take for someone who has spent "his youth whoring/after English gods" and he returns home. But there is yet another disillusionment to follow for home is no longer what it used to be, what far away in London he had loved and cherished in his memories. The political bondage over, a cultural bondage has taken its place:

> The hourglass of the Tamil mind
> is replaced by the exact chronometer
> of Europe. (*RP*, 22)

Then again,

> The sky is no different
> Beggars are the same everywhere. The clubs
> are there, complete with bar and golf-links. (*RP*, 23)

He has returned home only to find that the exile continues. Time has run its course leaving Parthasarathy all alone – uprooted and insecure, so that he exclaims: "What have I come/here for from a thousand miles?" (*RP*, 22) "The ashes are all that's left" of his youth and the other half of his life is yet to be lived. Whether it is England or India – wherever he goes he is all alone except with the women he loves.

The second section "Trial" celebrates love – the only force that helps overcome the feelings of alienation. In that it is a direct contrast to the first section. The dull grey colours of despondency and gloom in "Exile" give way to rainbows and gold in "Trial." Excitement takes over:

> Touch brings the body into focus,
> restores colour to inert hands,
>
> till the skin takes over
> erasing angularities, and the four walls
> turn on a strand of hair. (*RP*, 35)

Parthasarathy follows Ramanujan's example of writing about memories of the past:

Over the family album, the other night,
I shared your childhood:
the unruly hair silenced by bobpins

and ribbons, eyes half-shut
before the glass,
a ripple of arms round Suneeti's neck. . . . (*RP,* 30)

The experience is, however, just the opposite of Ramanujan's who regretted not being able to share his childhood with his wife.

Towards the end of "Trial" however, tensions have set in. Where "the heart isn't hospitable" (*RP,* 42) how long can one celebrate the body, "something so perishable, trite?" (*RP,* 38)

A major concern of Parthasarathy is the handling of the English language by Indians. Quite early in the first section "Exile," he states his own opinion on the use of a foreign language for creative writing:

language is a tree, loses colour
under another sky. (*RP,* 15)

The third section "Homecoming" opens with the poet's desire to give up English for Tamil. He finds himself bound in "English chains" but his hunger for his mother tongue is yet to be assuaged. But once again disappointment is in store for Parthasarathy. The classical Tamil, the "bull" of a bygone era

is today an unrecognizable carcass,
quick with the fleas of Kodambakkam. (*RP,* 48)

The only way out is to turn to the past and

strike out a line for yourself
from the iron of life's ordinariness. (*RP,* 48)

For "How long can foreign poets/provide the staple of your lines?" (*RP,* 48)

To continue with the theme developed in the first two sections, "Homecoming" delineates the event of 'the return of the native.' Although different in attitudes, a number of instances abound using situations, events and ironical remarks somewhat in the Ramanujan fashion. The description of a cousin –

> Sundari, who had squirrelled up and down
> forbidden tamarind trees in her long skirt
> every morning with me,
>
> stood there, that day, forty years taller,
> her three daughters floating
> like safe planets near her. (*RP*, 49)

is reminding of Ramanujan's "Looking for a Cousin on a Swing." (*SP*, 8) Again, Ramanujan's ironical remark on his father's death in "Obituary" may be compared with Parthasarathy's:

> I shall follow. And after me,
> my unborn son, through the eye of this needle
> of forgetfulness. (*RP*, 50)

The reflection of a stranger that Ramanujan draws in "Self-Portrait" (*SP*, 9) is also used by Parthasarathy:

> Often confront a stranger
> in the scratched glass, older perhaps,
> who resembles my father. (*RP*, 52)

They are undoubtedly different. But the influence of Ramanujan is much too obvious.

The rest of "Homecoming" is about the poet trying to come to terms with his circumstances:

> I have exchanged the world
> for a table and chair. I shouldn't complain. (*RP*, 56)

Strangely enough, the poems in this section do not mention his wife, children and others. There are only streets, traffic, unopened letters emphasizing his isolation. It is only in the concluding lines that he refers to his marriage and children and that too in a note of submission to fate:

> I've rolled my fate

into a paper ball and tossed it

out the window. I can now walk
to the end of the marriage
on my knees for my unspeaking sons. (*RP,* 63)

It is true that *Rough Passage* starts off as an attempt to overcome feelings of alienation. But the chief concern of the poet is a rediscovery of his own self, of what he has made of himself in love, in marriage and in poetry. The second edition ends on a note of resignation to be contented with life with its "small change of uncertainties." (*RP,* 61) But this should not be taken as final for Parthasarathy continues to add to this sequence of poems. It is for us to wait and watch whether the next edition alters the tone of the conclusion or allows it to remain as it is.

IV

Dom Moraes is an entirely different case. With him the circumstances and hence the problems of expatriation are different. His first sixteen years were spent in Bombay, whereafter he migrated to England and adopted British citizenship in 1961. Alienation in him is not a natural consequence that follows from the circumstances. Rather, it is, as Ajit Khullar puts it, "a willed alienation"[7]—a conscious decision on his part to leave India and settle abroad. The fact is that he takes pains to disown his Indian heritage:

> I am Indian by birth, but I have lived in England since I was a boy and I hold a British passport. The historical accident of British rule in India worked on my family so that I lived an English life there and spoke no Indian language. . . . So English was my outlook, I found I could not fit in India. When eventually I came to England I fitted in at once.[8]

There is the same cool determination in his poems relating to India, the country of his origin. Unwilling to enter, he watches the scene from a distance:

I saw my whole country,
A defeated dream

Hiding itself in prayers,
A population of corpses, . . .
Sorrow has stopped your eye.
Your dream is desolate.
It calls me everyday
But I cannot enter it.
You know I will not return.
Forgive me my trespasses.[9]

The poem deals with his feelings about his mother as well as his motherland. He refuses to settle down in India and opts for a poetic career in England and writes to his mother:

I am tidying my life
In this cold country. (*CP*, 99)

But this tidying requires a great deal of effort which Moraes finds himself incapable of. For soon he realizes the ambivalence of his predicament:

loose images fall at my heel.
No use to me, and so I leave them there.
Last August in the Valley of Jezreel,
Homesick, I dreamt about Trafalgar Square.

But in the Square today, I dream of hawks,
Of doelike girls, the sun, endless delay,
Bullocks and Buicks, statesmen like great auks,
And I grow homesick for an Indian day. (*CP*, 95)

However, Moraes does not seem to be obsessed by such feelings and there aren't many poems done around them. In fact they are never the central preoccupation of any of his poems. He makes passing references to them while discussing other topics. But in his autobiography he is quite explicit about this ambivalence:

> But the colours and smells of India, the emotions I had at Kanheri, the painful sort of affection I had for Kutthalingam all pulled me one way, and the new life I led abroad, with friends and work and a milieu I understood, more than I did India,

> pulled me the other.[10]

It is also interesting to note the sense of delight and pride that he has on observing that his son had something of Indianness in his looks:

> I cross the room to kiss my son, whose skin has an odour of baby soap and milk. He has English apples for cheeks, but somewhere behind them is a tinge of gold and olive, the colour of the country from which I came.[11]

V

Exile and feelings of expatriation are not themes as such in the works of Vikram Seth. But being continually on the move, and having spent considerable time in various countries there creeps in a sense of insecurity and loneliness which he frankly admits:

> Unsettledness
> Is what I have come to fear.[12]

The irony is that the feeling persists even when he is in India, at home. The sense of rootlessness eats from within:

> I envy those
> Who have a house of their own,
> Who can say their feet
> Rest on what is theirs alone,
> Who do not live on sufferance
> In stranger's shells,
> As my family has all our life,
> And as I probably will. (*HAG,* 37)

But such a mood is rare in Seth. He generally keeps a happy-go-lucky tone, happy with what comes and living each moment to its fullest with little time for looking back and lamenting. His acceptance of his lot as it is lends to his poems a different tone. A typical example is "Unclaimed" (*HAG,* 62) which proclaims the value of living on the surface of life, thereby avoiding all sorts of emotional and other complications:

To make love with a stranger is the best.
There is no riddle and there is no test.

Seth's attitude to life can be summarily summed up in the following lines:

There is so much to do
There isn't anytime for feeling blue.
There isn't any point in feeling sad.
Things could be worse. Right now they are only bad. (*HAG*, 58)

VI

There is, then, something of a tradition being built of expatriate Indian poetry. With Ramanujan paving the way and Parthasarathy following suit others have come in to provide variety of thought and feeling. With the number of people visiting foreign countries and even settling down there on the increase day by day one does expect this particular realm of Indian English poetry to gain both in quantity and quality. For all the charms of life abroad, 'Home, sweet Home' will continue to attract and inspire.

NOTES

1. R. Parthasarathy, *Rough Passage* (New Delhi: O.U.P., 1985), p. 15. Hereafter *RP*.
2. A.K. Ramanujan, *Selected Poems* (New Delhi: O.U.P., 1976), p. 25. Hereafter *SP*.
3. R. Parthasarathy, "How it Strikes a Contemporary?: The Poetry of Ramanujan," *Osmania Journal of English Studies,* no. XIII, p. 193.
4. M.K. Naik, "A.K. Ramanujan and the Search for Roots," *Dimensions of Indian English Literature* (New Delhi, Sterling), p. 21.
5. T.S. Eliot, "Tradition and Individual Talent," *The Sacred Wood*

(London: Methuen, 1950), p. 54.

6. Bruce King, *Modern Indian Poetry in English* (Oxford University Press, 1987), p. 212.
7. Ajit Khullar, "Willed Alienation," *Indian Literature,* vol. XXXII no. 3, 1989, p. 137.
8. Dom Moraes, "Shall I Paint Myself White?" *Impact: Asian Views of the West,* ed. Jo Ann White (New York, 1971), pp. 183-84.
9. Dom Moraes, *Collected Poems* (New Delhi: Penguin India, 1990), p. 100. Hereafter, *CP.*
10. Dom Moraes, *My Son's Father* (New Delhi: Penguin India, 1990), p. 164.
11. *Ibid.*, p. 242.
12. Vikram Seth, *The Humble Administrator's Garden* (New Delhi: O.U.P., 1987), p. 25. Hereafter *HAG.*

Expatriate Experience in the Writings of Sri Paramahansa Yogananda

K.V. RAMA RAO

Hail, Mother of religions, lotus, scenic beauty, and sages!
Thy wide doors are open,
Welcoming God's true sons through all ages.
Where Ganges, woods, Himalayan caves, and men dream God –
I am hallowed; my body touched that sod.[1]

What a blessedness it could be to an expatriate Indian to die with these words on his lips! Yogananda had often said: "I do not wish to die in bed, but with my boots on, speaking of God and India." And that is exactly how he entered Mahasamadhi on March 7, 1952, after speaking in a public meeting at Biltmore Hotel, Los Angeles, arranged in honour of the first Indian Ambassador to America. That was the glorious culmination of a successful career spanning over three decades in the west.

During the early years of his American life, Yogananda was confused as well as enthused by certain aspects of the American life. One day while riding to the seashore in Massachusetts, he noticed some "Hot Dog" sign-boards. Then he prayed: "My Lord, why did you bring me to the land where people eat dogs?" He asked a man what was inside those mysterious bags and the man replied "pork and beef." Then the Swami was reassured. On another occasion, he was astonished to see a new house, erected within a few hours' time. 'When I think of such energy, I like to be an American,' he says. Absorbing the good qualities in all the countries he visited, Sri Yogananda became a true citizen of the world. Yet, India was the darling of his heart.

Is this love of mine blind sentiment

That sees not the pathways of reason?
Ah, no! I love India,
for, there I learned first to love God and all things beautiful.
(191)

In 1920, at his guru's behest, Sri Yogananda accepted an invitation to represent India at the International Congress of Religious Liberals in Boston. Later, he was invited to stay on and give lectures and conduct classes in Yoga. Thousands became his followers. He founded the International Headquarters of his mission atop Mt. Washington in Los Angeles in 1925. He was invited by President Coolidge to the White House in 1927. But for a brief spell of less than two years when he revisited India during 1935-36, he spent the rest of his life there in America. He published his magnum opus *Autobiography of a Yogi* in 1946.

While in India before his first departure to the West, the Himalayas had a great fascination for Yogananda. Many times he tried to reach the mighty arms of the magnificent Himalayas. But only once he visited them and he enjoyed himself thoroughly. But the beauty, grandeur and sacredness of the Himalayas is a recurrent theme in his poems and his *Autobiography.* "In Me," he sings:

O huge Himalaya
With snowy sovereign white regalia!
In my mind doth rest thy throne –
Thy home in me, in me. (99)

Yogananda had seen many parts of the world and he loved all places, as he loved all people as the children of one God. But, India had a niche in his heart. As a child he loved his mother very dearly. Her big large dark eyes had a magnetic attraction for him. When he lost his mother in his eleventh year, he wept bitterly. He was inconsolable for a long time. He smote the doors of Heaven with his intense prayers, till the Mother of Cosmos spoke to him and revealed the reality of human fragility and permanency of divine love. His poems "Two Black Eyes" and "My Mother's Eyes" reveal at once the human and the divine sides of the poet's personality.

Many a time
By bitter speech and sadness driven,

The boat of my life found safety
In the harbor of those two eyes.
And now the cruel death-quake has forever marred
Those dream-harboring eyes. (103)

Just as an earthquake can destabilize the safety of a harbor, so the shelter of his mother's eyes was destroyed by the death-quake. His dreams were shattered. Finally the cloud-voice of Mother Divine assured him that it was she who had loved him in the form of many mothers through many incarnations.

"My Native Land" is an enchanting lyric in which Yogananda pays homage to India for the little pleasures of an earthly paradise and for teaching him true hove:

The friendly sky,
Inviting shade of banyan tree,
The holy Ganges flowing by–
How can I forget thee!

For all this, Yogananda is not a romantic sentimentalist to feed on nostalgic memories and thoughts always. On discovering the hill-top mansion of Mt. Washington, he declares:

Jehovah! This is the land of solace
Where my life's dream in truth reappears!

He is a true yogi, really untouched by external circumstances. He is at home everywhere. During the course of a lecture Yogananda observes: "By constant communion with Him, everything but God vanishes. I have no consciousness of nationality, no consciousness of India or America. I love you all just as I love my own family. Good or bad, I love all alike, or they are my brothers and sisters. Naughty or good, we are His children."[2]

Thus, a study of the works of Paramahansa Yogananda adds a new dimension to the theme of expatriate experience. For, according to sages, we are exiles in this world. The World of Reality is beyond this phenomenal world. This world is a dream. It is not our home. The true home, the fatherland, is elsewhere. All of us, without exception, consciously or unconsciously, are on the Homeward journey! The poet compares himself to a beautiful bird. Let us observe its symbolic journey:

> With living threads of Thy beauty, my winsome wings were woven. Endowed with a spark of immortality, I have flown from life to life. I escape from all who audaciously try to possess me; I belong only to Thee. No transiency enthralls me; my true Home is Thy changeless spirit.
>
> Thou hast clothed barren eternity in the verdure of multi-coloured cycle. In the forest of incarnations, I flit gaily from tree to tree. I shall alight at last, O Lord, upon Thine out-stretched hand.[3]

It is because Sri Yogananda spoke so lovingly and with such conviction about God that he was accepted as a great religious leader in the west. Robert S. Ellwood, Chairman, School of Religion, University of Southern California observes: "Yogananda has become an image – a remarkable, deep, sweet, poetic, ecstatic man enraptured of cosmic life – who has changed the map of American religious life."[4] Coming from such a learned and authoritative man such as Robert Ellwood, it is no mean tribute to the glorious life of this darling son of India, who worked as her cultural ambassador through his mighty mission in all the countries of the world.

While issuing a commemorative stamp in his honour in March 1977, the Government of India paid homage to this great Master, in these words: "The ideal of love for god and service to humanity found full expression in the life of Paramahansa Yogananda. Though the major part of his life was spent outside India, still he takes his place among our great saints."

NOTES

1. Paramahansa Yogananda, *Songs of the Soul* (Los Angeles, California: Self-Realization Fellowship, 1983), pp. 168-71.
2. Paramahansa Yogananda, *The Divine Romance* (Los Angeles, S.R.F., 1986), p. 261.
3. Paramahansa Yogananda, *Whispers from Eternity* (Calcutta: Dakshineswar, 1982), p. 63.
4. Paramahansa Yogananda, *Where There is Light* (Los Angeles: Self-Realization Fellowship, 1989), cover.

Budha Behind the Bottles: Meddegama's Experience in America

A.J. JOSE ALILAKUZHY

Udaya Prasanta Meddegama, the Sri Lankan Sinhalese poet, has written quite a few English poems, some of which have been published in the collection *Nothing but a Dream.*[1] His instincts of observation are as cannibalistic as it might be with any poet alive to his age and in an easy personal stance he reveals his disillusionment in a dreamland – the country of his choice. He is not shy or afraid to muscle in on his most intimate relationship and bare himself. Here is a feast of the poet's experiences in an alien country. The disarming simplicity and artlessness of the poems stun the reader at a time when literature is made as complicated and incomprehensible as life itself.

The attitude of the poet is sure to be influenced by the cause of his migration to the country of his choice. In the poem "Disillusionment," he tells us the reason why he went to America.

> Full of hope
> I crossed
> the seven seas
> looking for
> the pot of gold. (14)

It is hard for a man to admit that he was lured by money to a country, especially for a man from the East, for material gains and worldly prosperity are looked down upon in this part of the world. Here Meddegama is not taking the position of the millions who swarm to the richest country in the world. Taking us into confidence he is speaking the truth, his truth, unlike the scores of Indian and other Eastern writers who have settled in that dreamland. The poet here is in no urgency to justify himself for abandoning his country and staying elsewhere. His approach is purely that of a professional and we begin to doubt whether such a person can write poetry. But soon from the very poem we learn that

> now this vast land
> of pleasure and luck
> seems to be
> a graveyard. (14)

The disillusionment is not due to the poet's failure to make money but is effected by the winter that brings life to a stand-still. He finds hungry squirrels and neglected birds hovering in dead trees.

> The sky sigh
> The ground murmurs
> The trees sob
> The wind moans. (14)

To Meddegama whose mind is full of the memories of an always warm country with evergreen trees full of fruits and with happy squirrels and birds on them, the snow-covered, lifeless New York in the winter is a graveyard. The climatic difference is an obsession with the poet and America is always associated with images of winter and lifelessness. The poem "Nostalgia" presents a direct contrast between the winter in America and the warmth in Sri Lanka:

> But here in New York
> flocks of brown birds
> shivering and baffled
> Soaring above the snow
> as if looking for the grass
> hidden under the white carpet . . .
> Over there in Sri Lanka
> Evergreen trees
> full of fruit and flowers
> singing birds and dancing squirrels
> fleshy and juicy mangoes
> golden bananas and pineapples
> and – green, green grass, green leafy trees. (9)

"Nostalgia" is not a children's poem that illustrates the climatic difference between a tropical country and a cold one. Winter and the dullness created by the days passing slowly and reluctantly accompanied by wind and snow are only situations that compelled him to write this poem. The poem is more about the "twelve months of sweat and love" that he left behind, than about the twelve months of fruits and flowers as we see in the last line of the poem. It is the agony of a soul in an alien land and its yearning to be back among the familiar that is revealed here. And it is the shift from the apparent to the deeper feelings that makes Meddegama's verses poetry and him a poet.

The alienation and the sense of an emptiness that expands within are expressed in the poem "Standing on Route 14." The poet is waiting on route 14, opposite the Seneca Lake and watching it and he loses the sense of time. After a long time suddenly it dawns upon him that the route is abandoned, the lake is scary and the chapel rising above the trees is haunted. Soon

> A big dog
> with a black rounded snout
> dashing out of
> a fraternity house
> joins me
> standing on route 14
> We begin to fathom
> the lake
> with the long lines
> of our glances (15)

He finds himself in a deserted street with only a strange dog to measure the time and the depth of the lake. One wonders how alienation, emptiness and misery can be expressed better.

The "Sunday Dream" is an escape from the dull monotony and lifeless existence. The vast emptiness that spreads on all sides compels him to go to office even on a Sunday. No coffee is available, no beer, it is a rest day even for the vending machines. Office is a blissful place because he could do some work and escape the thoughts of his land and the people. Some few moments later the poet slides into an oriental dream in which he sees swans and red lotuses in the Seneca Lake.

I call out to the brown girl
with long black eyes and braids. . . .
She beckons and
Unable to resist her alluring smile
How could I, ever reach her? (6)

Meddegama is trying to be among the like-minded, like-coloured people. He remains a foreigner and yearns for the company of a brown girl. If it is impossible in real life he will have it in a dream. But the disillusionment is even more painful than the boredom, once he wakes up.

I wake up
in my office in Demarest
amidst text books and lecture notes
and a pile of used disposable cups (6)

The still more painful monotony is revealed in the whiteness of snow and that of the thousands of cars moving in the streets.

As I look out of the window
There is still
a light snowfall
thousands of cars
All painted
pure white –
cute Machines. (6)

It is the mind of Meddegama that carries with it the warmth and love of Sri Lanka that generates this alienation. All the dreams of the east have to be wiped out of his mind for him to accept the realities of the present and be happy. He has to destroy – not forget – his brown identity and become part of the life and culture there. He has to go out of himself and live an Amerian life. In his poem "Snow," he writes:

'Father, let's go out'
My daughters insist
'Children, how could we trample
those soft feathers?' (13)

Though he is fighting shy of the American culture he wishes to permeate the snow, to leave behind the burden and to feel light, and fly away into the oblivion. He wants to dissolve himself into the American culture and disappear like a pinch of sugar put in a glass of water.

> Children I come
> We'll play in the snow
> Don't step on it
> We'll fly over it
> – with it – yes
> Let's be part of it
> And we'll disappear
> with snow
> Like snow (13)

It seems that there are sweeping moments when he forgets himself and becomes a nothing or nobody. "How Sad is this Dream of a Dream – Chikamatsu" presents such a situation that creates utter confusion in the poet's mind:

> From the dream world
> smiling, joyfully, hopefully
> we migrate
> into another dream world
> then peeping into
> each other's eyes,
> and sometimes
> into one's own reflection
> We wonder
> Who are we?
> Are we real? (38)

But no! The poet is never capable of that self-denial and the merger is never complete. The awareness of his true identity forces itself out of him in the poem "We, Sinhalese."

> We are the lords
> of the pearl
> of the Indian Ocean

the paradise
in the east
We are the proud
descendants of the lion
We don't care for tomorrow. (45)

Apart from the abstract feelings that remain basic to his experiences and poetry, there are concrete events that create aversion and even hatred to America. The poet believed that he was going to a paradise to find "the wishing tree" that fulfils all his desires, while going to the new land. The experiences were in stark contrast with the picture in his mind.

But we are in a paradise
of hatred,
corruption, lust
and
overwhelming ignorance. (16)

We learn about gleaming cars moving very fast carrying diseases never heard before. The more shocking awareness is that they sometimes poison medicaments to kill innocent children. The land of gold, the heaven of the poor in the East appears to be a crazy world to Meddegama. All the values are standing on the head and make a father miserable in the poem "A Child Watching T.V. in America."

My ten year old daughter
watches with interest
a T.V. program on
'Children having children'
and wonders how. (16)

Meddegama discovers only a filthy and shallow life, in the pleasure-hunting world. The people are always rushing to work, to earn time and money to live and enjoy. In "Here and There," he writes:

Nice guys here
with their broad grins
in the rush
saying Hi and Bye

round the clock
Moving eternally
like comets. (18)

The poet from Sri Lanka knows that all this haste is for nothing because he comes from a land where people coolly read horoscope even in bed "waiting for auspicious moments to copulate."

Even to death
they dont rush
because they know
death is just like
changing trains. (19)

In the land of plenty, life is a carnival with festival after festival. The shopkeepers sell kites, paper dolls, hot dogs, pop corns and dreams. They cater to every need of the consumer and consumerism rules the roost. In "Festivals," he writes:

First it was Halloween
followed by thanksgiving
Christmas and New Year arriving soon,
What's now
Valentine's – for love and happiness!
How nice!
So many festivals
for drinking and dancing. (20)

The foolishness, hypocrisy and snobbery of the American intellectuals irritate him as much as the meaningless practises of the common man. He lashes out at the pseudo-intellectuals in the "Intellectuals:"

How foolish are
these intellectuals!
How they toil
in Europe or America
to earn
more and more Certificates
Colourful robes;

and hats of all odd shapes. (31)

They continue to stooge, gossip, boast and scheme like intellectuals not knowing how little they really know.

"Dr. Baker" is a poem that illustrates the fate of an intellectual. He has contributed inventions and controversial theories in his time. Now all the aura and glory have gone and he is seen struggling in and out of the car and moving across the road dragging his feet. The poet asks the lonely old man:

Is it only the mailman
Who is still aware
of your existence? . . .
the walking stick
your last companion. (11-12)

His wife died thirty years ago and his daughter and son have other things to do. If this is the fate of Dr. Baker, born and brought up in America what will come to him!

One of the most painful experiences Meddegama confronts is related with his religious faith. In "Guess Who is Behind the Bottles," the poet's daughter forgets the small idol of Budha on her table after two weeks in America. As she has no time to decorate the image with flowers everyday and because it is difficult to get real flowers in winter, she has got paper flowers for her Budha. The children are more interested in the He Man, Spider Man or the Bat Man than in Budha. One evening Anne takes him to Cosie, her Italian friend. The nice man squeezes Anne's cheeks, offers a free drink and takes out a bronze Budha from behind the bottles in his bar. It was gifted by another man from the land of Budha and tea:

"I am so proud
to have this Budha
in my bar,
I rub his belly
and ask for luck,
He really helps me sometimes,"
Says the Barman aloud
Holding the Budha between two fingers
like a piece of cheese.

"Is that how you people
use the Budha in your country?" (2)

Meddegama remains speechless as the barman shoves the small image back behind the bottles like an empty bottle after rubbing his belly and kissing his head. Lord Budha has become a consumer item that you use and throw. The poet doesn't easily recover from the shock. He asks god,

Oh! Lord,
What are you doing here
in Cosie's bar? (2)

It is a question that the poet asks himself. What is he doing in America, where there is every possibility of his being thrown out after use? Where his religion is insulted, where human values are trampled what can an Eastern poet do? It is better to escape the contamination and save his family from the infection.

"Before Long" is a poem that describes his return journey.

Child, don't worry
You wont be cold for long
We are going back. . . .
Lets go home
Back to poverty
Mosquitoes and flies. (22-23)

In the homeland there may be poverty, but it is the homeland and he can escape his daughter's question whether he kissed her mother's lips like the man in the film and how it tasted. The child may miss the rubber spiders in the cereal packets, but she would be able to see the real, beautiful and poisonous ones. A walk in the hot evening under the Mara trees will comfort her.

Let us go back to a statement that I made in the beginning of this article that the attitude of a person to the country and his expatriate experiences is determined by the cause of his migration. Meddegama is not a refugee in America and nothing can force upon him the culture that he doesn't cherish. Even after going to the Unites States he has the freedom of choice to select from the two and he opts for the familiar. A highly sensitive poet cannot easily overcome the alienation, emptiness and nostalgia.

NOTE

1. Udaya Prasanta Meddegama, *Nothing but a Dream* (Sri Lanka: University of Peradenia, 1988).

Index